BBC goodfood

ULTIMATE UNPROCESSED RECIPES

EDITOR
Ailsa Burt

BBC
BOOKS

BBC Books, an imprint of Ebury Publishing
20 Vauxhall Bridge Road
London SW1V 2SA

BBC Books is part of the Penguin Random House group of companies whose addresses can be found at global.penguinrandomhouse.com

Photographs © BBC Magazines 2024
Recipes © BBC Worldwide 2024
Book Design © Woodlands Books Ltd 2024

All recipes contained in this book first appeared in *BBC Good Food Magazine*

First published by BBC Books in 2024

www.penguin.co.uk

A CIP catalogue record for this book is available from the British Library

ISBN 9781785949326

Project Editors: Kay Halsey and Katie Fisher
Commissioning Editor: Nell Warner
Cover Design: Two Associates
Design: Clarkevanmeurs Design
Picture Research: Gabby Harrington
With thanks to Ailsa Burt and Vyki Hendy

Printed and bound in Germany by Mohn Media Mohndruck GmbH

The authorised representative in the EEA is Penguin Random House Ireland, Morrison Chambers, 32 Nassau Street, Dublin D02 YH68.

Penguin Random House is committed to a sustainable future for our business, our readers and our planet. This book is made from Forest Stewardship Council® certified paper.

PICTURE AND RECIPE CREDITS

BBC Books would like to thank the following people for providing photos. While every effort has been made to trace and acknowledge all photographers, we would like to apologise should there be any errors or omissions in the following.

Mike English 11, 22, 31, 43, 45, 48, 53, 55, 61, 74, 77, 85, 87, 91, 95, 99, 105, 107, 109, 111, 119, 121, 125, 129, 130, 133, 145, 147, 149, 163, 169, 185, 195, 211, 217; Hannah Taylor-Eddington 17, 27, 35, 37, 41, 57, 93, 219; Stuart Ovenden 33, 51, 67, 123, 127, 157, 165, 171; Will Heap 15, 21, 63, 83, 139, 209; Tom Regester 79, 97, 177, 187, 215; David Munns 117, 152, 155, 173, 191; Rob Streeter 47, 71, 143, 207, 221; Myles New 6, 19, 160, 196, 203; Peter Cassidy 69, 179, 199, 205; Faith Mason 73, 115, 167; Jonathan Gregson 135, 174, 193; Melissa Reynolds-James 13, 201; Yuki Sugiura 59, 213; Hayley Benoit 103, 113; Maja Smend 141, 183; Jean Cazals 25; Gareth Morgans 29; Simon Wheeler 39; Karen Thomas 65; Kris Kirkham 89; Ella Miller 137; Emma Boyns 151; Sam Stowell 159; Clare Winfield 181; Louise Hagger 189.

All the recipes in this book were created by the editorial team at *Good Food* and by regular contributors to BBC Magazines.

Contents

Introduction

Are you looking to limit your intake of ultra-processed foods, or UPFs? Being aware of UPFs and taking steps to limit your consumption of them will help your health and diet in the long run.

There are four levels of food processing and to some degree, most food items, except for whole fruits and vegetables, are processed. This doesn't necessarily mean they're bad for you, for example, milk is pasteurised to eliminate any harmful bacteria and make it safe for us to drink. However, UPFs are foods that have been highly modified, removing almost all nutritional value. And they are designed to be hyper-palatable, so you crave them more. UPFs are commonly found in items like ready meals, packaged biscuits, cakes and breads, cereals, crisps, sausages, hot dogs, burgers, fizzy drinks, chocolate, confectionery and lots of ready-to-heat products. A good rule of thumb is to scour the packaging and look at the ingredients. Are you unsure what all the ingredients are? Are there more than a handful of ingredients? If the answer is yes, it is probably a UPF. For this book, we have defined UPFs using the NOVA food classification system, with those in Category 4 being ultra-processed foods.

There are also tricky foods to classify, for example, peanut butter. If it's made purely from nuts or nuts and salt, then it's not classed as a UPF, but when sugars, oils, preservatives and artificial additives are mixed in, then it is classed as a UPF. Always try to buy the best quality you can afford and check the packet ingredients if unsure.

In this book, we've included a helpful Make Your Own chapter, where you will find how to cook homemade versions of common UPFs. And throughout the book, there are better alternatives to pre-packaged breakfasts, lunches, freezer foods and ready meals.

You'll find quick and healthy lunches to pack up for work, some familiar favourites for families and easy dishes to knock together for entertaining. You'll even find a Batch Cooking chapter to make those evenings when you feel like reaching for convenience food a thing of the past. All have been rigorously tested in the *Good Food* test kitchen, so you can rest easy that they will work first time around.

Happy cooking!

Ailsa Burt, Editor

Notes & Conversion Tables

NOTES ON THE RECIPES
- Eggs are large in the UK and Australia and extra large in America unless stated.
- Wash fresh produce before preparation.
- Recipes contain nutritional analyses for 'sugar', which means the total sugar content including all natural sugars in the ingredients, unless otherwise stated.

APPROXIMATE LIQUID CONVERSIONS

Metric	Imperial	AUS	US
50ml	2fl oz	¼ cup	¼ cup
125ml	4fl oz	½ cup	½ cup
175ml	6fl oz	¾ cup	¾ cup
225ml	8fl oz	1 cup	1 cup
300ml	10fl oz/½ pint	½ pint	1¼ cups
450ml	16fl oz	2 cups	2 cups/1 pint
600ml	20fl oz/1 pint	1 pint	2½ cups
1 litre	35fl oz/1¾ pints	1¾ pints	1 quart

APPROXIMATE WEIGHT CONVERSIONS
- Cup measurements, which are used in Australia and America, have not been listed here as they vary from ingredient to ingredient. Kitchen scales should be used to measure dry, solid ingredients.

OVEN TEMPERATURES

GAS	°C	°C FAN	°F	OVEN TEMP.
¼	110	90	225	Very cool
½	120	100	250	Very cool
1	140	120	275	Cool or slow
2	150	130	300	Cool or slow
3	160	140	325	Warm
4	180	160	350	Moderate
5	190	170	375	Moderately hot
6	200	180	400	Fairly hot
7	220	200	425	Hot
8	230	210	450	Very hot
9	240	220	475	Very hot

SPOON MEASURES
Spoon measurements are level unless otherwise specified.
- 1 teaspoon (tsp) = 5ml
- 1 tablespoon (tbsp) = 15ml
- 1 Australian tablespoon = 20ml (cooks in Australia should measure 3 teaspoons where 1 tablespoon is specified in a recipe)

Good Food is concerned about sustainable sourcing and animal welfare. Where possible, humanely reared meats, sustainably caught fish (see fishonline.org for further information from the Marine Conservation Society) and free-range chickens and eggs are used when recipes are originally tested.

Chapter 1:
MAKE YOUR OWN

These recipes are a great alternative to the versions you can buy in store, and they are free from UPFs to boot.

Vegetable stock

A staple in any kitchen and free of UPFs, why not give making your own stock a go. This can be made with vegetable peelings and offcuts – simply store in the freezer until needed.

PREP 5 mins   COOK 2 hrs   MAKES 1 litre

- 4 celery sticks, cut into chunks
- 2 leeks, cut into chunks
- 2 carrots, cut into chunks
- 1 onion, skin on, cut into quarters
- 2 garlic cloves, bashed
- 1 star anise
- 5 peppercorns
- bouquet garni of 2 parsley stalks, 2 sprigs of thyme and 1 bay leaf, tied with kitchen string

1 Tip everything into a large saucepan with a pinch of salt, then cover with 2 litres of water. Bring to the boil, then reduce to a simmer and cook for 2 hrs. Pass through a sieve and use for your intended recipe. Will keep in the fridge for a week and for 6 months in the freezer.

Nutrition per 100ml serving:
Kcals 18, fat 1g, saturates 0.3g, carbs 0.4g, sugars 0.3g, fibre 0.3g, protein 1.5g, salt 0.08g

Chicken stock

Essential in cooking and without any UPFs, this homemade stock recipe gives a great depth to any stew or soup. You can mix up the veg you add to give different flavours.

 PREP 5 mins   COOK 3 hrs   MAKES 1 litre

- 1kg chicken carcasses or wings
- 1 carrot, cut into chunks
- 1 onion, skin on, cut into quarters
- 1 leek, cut into chunks
- 1 celery stick, cut into chunks
- 1 garlic clove, bashed
- bouquet garni of 2 parsley stalks, 2 sprigs of thyme and 1 bay leaf, tied with kitchen string
- 5 peppercorns
- 1 clove

1 Tip everything into a large saucepan with a pinch of salt, then cover with 2 litres of water. Bring to the boil, then reduce to a simmer and cook for 3 hrs, skimming when needed. Pass through a sieve and use for your intended recipe. Will keep in the fridge for a week and for 3 months in the freezer.

TIP
You can store any chicken carcasses leftover from roasts in the freezer until needed to make stock.

Nutrition per 100ml serving:
Kcals 18, fat 1g, saturates 0.3g, carbs 0.4g, sugars 0.3g, fibre 0.3g, protein 1.5g, salt 0.08g

Slow-cooker bone broth

Energy efficient and hands off, start this bone broth off on a Saturday morning and by Sunday lunchtime it's done. Minimal effort for a deeply fragrant and flavourful broth.

🕐 PREP 30 mins   COOK 36 hrs   🍴 4

- 1kg mixture of beef or veal bones and/or chicken, ask your butcher what they have
- 2 carrots, roughly chopped
- 1 leek, roughly chopped
- 1 celery stick, roughly chopped
- 1 lemon, juiced
- 1 bay leaf

1 Heat the oven to 180C/160C fan/gas 4. Spread the bones out on a baking sheet and roast them for an hour, turning them over after 30 mins.

2 Heat the slow cooker if necessary. Pack the veg into the slow cooker, add the bones and enough water to fill the pot to within 2cm of the top. Add the lemon juice and the bay leaf. Cover and cook on Low for 18–36 hours. The longer you cook the broth the darker it will become.

3 Put a colander over a bowl and scoop out all the bones into the colander. Return any broth from the bowl to the pan. Strain all the liquid through a fine sieve. Taste, and season only if you need to. Allow the broth to cool and lift off the fat. Store in the fridge for up to 3 days or transfer to freezer bags once it has cooled. Will keep for 3 months in the freezer.

Nutrition per serving:
Kcals 45, fat 0.3g, saturates 0.1g, carbs 4g, sugars 2g, fibre 0.2g, protein 6g, salt 0.6g

Tortillas

A lot of bread is mass produced and offers very little in the way of nutrients. Making your own tortillas is surprisingly easy and once you've tried homemade, you won't go back!

🕐 PREP 30 mins plus resting   COOK 25 mins   🥧 Makes 6 tortillas

- 250g plain flour, plus a little more for dusting
- 2 tbsp cold pressed sunflower oil
- ½ tsp fine salt

1 Combine the flour, vegetable oil and salt in a bowl. Pour over 150ml warm water and knead to bring the mixture together. Remove from the bowl and knead on a lightly floured work surface for around 5 mins until you make a soft, smooth ball of dough. Cover with a clean tea towel and rest for at least 15 mins before rolling out.

2 Cut the dough into 6 equal pieces (about 75g each). Roll out each ball of dough as thinly as possible on a floured work surface. They should make rounds about 20cm wide, 2mm thick.

3 Heat a large frying pan over a medium–high heat. Cook the tortillas for 1–2 mins on each side until golden brown and toasted. Wrap them in foil and cover in a tea towel to keep warm, while you cook the rest. Keeps for 2 days well wrapped, or cool, wrap and freeze for up to 3 months.

Nutrition per tortilla:
Kcals 187, fat 4g, saturates 0g, carbs 32g, sugars 0g, fibre 2g, protein 4g, salt 0.4g

Pitta bread

These are easy to rustle up, great to make ahead and free from any UPFs. They freeze well so make a big batch for easy dinners and snacks.

PREP 20 mins plus rising   COOK 40 mins   Makes 8 pittas

- 2 tsp fast-action dried yeast
- 500g strong white bread flour, plus extra for dusting
- 2 tsp salt
- 1 tbsp olive oil

1 Mix the yeast with 300ml warm water in a large bowl. Leave to sit for 5 mins until the yeast is super bubbly then tip in the flour, salt and oil. Bring the mixture together into a soft dough. Don't worry if it looks a little rough round the edges.

2 Tip the dough onto a lightly floured work surface. Knead for 5–10 mins until you have a soft, smooth and elastic dough. Try to knead using as little extra flour as possible, just enough so that the dough doesn't stick – this will keep the pittas light and airy. Once kneaded, place in a lightly oiled bowl, cover with a tea towel and leave to double in size, approximately 1 hour.

3 Heat the oven as high as it will go (ideally 250C/230C fan/gas 9) and put a large baking tray on the middle shelf of the oven to get searingly hot. Divide the dough into 8 balls, then flatten each into a disc with the palm of your hand. On a lightly floured surface, roll each disc into an oval, around 20cm long, 15cm wide and 3–5mm thick.

4 Carefully remove the hot tray from the oven. Dust with flour, then place your pittas directly onto it – you may have to do this in batches. Return swiftly to the oven and bake for 4–5 mins, or until the pittas have puffed up and are a pale golden colour. Wrap each hot pitta in a clean tea towel once it's baked to keep it soft while the others cook. Store in the freezer for up to 3 months.

Nutrition per pitta:
Kcals 246, fat 2g, saturates 0.4g, carbs 47g, sugars 0.3g, fibre 2g, protein 8g, salt 1g

Seedy brown loaf

Most standard sliced loaves you find in the supermarket are filled with additives to last longer, making them UPFs. This loaf freezes well sliced for excellent sandwiches all week.

🕐 PREP 20 mins plus rising   COOK 30 mins   ◔ Makes 1 loaf

- 400g malted grain brown bread flour or wholemeal or granary bread flour
- 100g strong white bread flour, plus extra for dusting
- 7g sachet fast-action dried yeast (or 2 tsp quick dried yeast)
- 1½ tsp salt
- 1 tbsp butter, softened, plus extra for the tin
- 4 tbsp mixed seeds, such as linseed, pumpkin, sesame and sunflower, plus extra for sprinkling (optional)

1 Mix the flours, yeast and salt in a large bowl. Add the butter and rub it into the flour. Stir in the seeds, if using. Make a dip in the centre and pour in almost 300ml hand warm (cool rather than hot) water. Mix with a round-bladed knife, adding a bit more water if needed, until the mixture comes together as a soft, not too sticky, dough. Gather into a ball.

2 Put the dough on a lightly floured surface and knead for 8–10 mins until smooth and elastic, only adding extra flour if necessary to prevent sticking. Cover with a glass bowl and leave for 45 mins–1 hr until doubled in size and it feels light and springy. Knock back the dough by lightly kneading 3–4 times. You only want to knock out large air bubbles and too much handling will lose the dough's lightness. Shape into a ball, cover with the bowl and leave for 15 mins.

3 Butter a 1.2-litre loaf tin (about 23 x 13 x 5.5cm) and line the base with baking parchment. Using your knuckles, flatten the dough into a 25 x 19cm rectangle. Fold the short ends into the centre like an envelope, make a ¼ turn, then flatten into the same size and roll up very tightly, starting from one of the short ends. Roll the top of the dough in extra seeds and place in the tin with the join underneath, pressing the seeds gently in. Cover with a clean tea towel. Leave for 40–45 mins, or until risen 5cm above the tin's top.

4 Put a tin in the bottom of the oven 20 mins before baking and heat the oven to 230C/210C fan/gas 8. Add the bread, pour 250ml cold water into the heated tin (this will hiss and create a burst of steam to give you a crisp crust), then lower the heat to 220C/200C fan/gas 7. Bake for 30 mins or until golden, covering with foil for the last 5 mins if browning too quickly. Leave in the tin for 2–3 mins, then remove and cool on a wire rack. If you tap the underneath of the loaf, it should be firm and sound hollow. Leave to cool completely before slicing. Will keep in the freezer for up to 3 months.

Nutrition per slice (20 slices):
Kcals 91, fat 1g, saturates 0g, carbs 18g, sugars 1g, fibre 1g, protein 3g, salt 0.38g

Easy bread rolls

Bake these rolls for sandwiches, burger buns or to dunk in soup. For burger buns, divide into 6 instead of 8 and scatter with sesame seeds. For hotdog buns, roll into finger shapes.

🕐 PREP 30 mins plus rising   COOK 30 mins   ◔ Makes 8 rolls

- 500g strong white bread flour, plus extra for dusting
- 7g sachet fast-action dried yeast
- 1 tsp caster sugar
- 2 tsp fine salt
- 1 tsp cold pressed sunflower oil, plus extra for the work surface and bowl

1 Tip the flour, yeast, sugar, salt and oil into a bowl. Pour over 325ml warm water, then mix (with a spatula or your hand), until it comes together as a shaggy dough. Make sure all the flour has been incorporated. Cover and leave for 10 mins.

2 Lightly oil your work surface and tip the dough onto it. Knead the dough for at least 10 mins until it becomes tighter and springy – if you have a stand mixer, you can do this with a dough hook for 5 mins. Pull the dough into a ball and put in a clean, oiled bowl. Leave for 1 hr, or until doubled in size.

3 Tip the dough onto a lightly floured surface and roll into a long sausage shape. Halve the dough, then divide each half into 4 pieces, so you have 8 equal-sized portions. Roll each into a tight ball and put on a dusted baking tray, leaving some room between each ball for rising. Cover with a damp tea towel and leave in a warm place to prove for 40 mins–1 hr or until almost doubled in size.

4 Heat the oven to 230C/210C fan/gas 8. When the dough is ready, dust each ball with a bit more flour. (If you like, you can glaze the rolls with milk or beaten egg, and top with seeds.) Bake for 25–30 mins, until light brown and hollow sounding when tapped on the base. Leave to cool on a wire rack. Will keep in an airtight container for up to 3 days or in the freezer for up to 3 months.

Nutrition per roll:
Kcals 246, fat 2g, saturates 0g, carbs 48g, sugars 1g, fibre 2g, protein 8g, salt 1.2g

Naan bread

Make your own Indian flatbreads at home and you'll never go back to buying them. Delicious eaten warm, these naans are ideal served with your favourite curry.

PREP 20 mins plus rising   COOK 35 mins   Makes 6–8 naan

- 7g sachet fast-action dried yeast
- 2 tsp golden caster sugar
- 300g strong white bread flour, plus extra for dusting
- ½ tsp baking powder
- 25g butter, melted, plus 2–3 tbsp for the bowl and brushing
- 150ml natural yogurt
- 1 tbsp nigella seeds

1 Put 125ml warm water into a bowl and sprinkle over the yeast and 1 tsp of the sugar. Leave for 10–15 mins or until frothy. In a larger bowl, put the flour, remaining sugar, ½ tsp salt and baking powder. Mix together, then make a well in the centre in which to pour the melted butter, yogurt, nigella seeds and yeast mixture. Stir well, then start to bring the mixture together with your hands. If it's very wet add a spoonful of flour but if it's dry add a splash more warm water. It should be a very soft dough but not so wet that it won't come together into a ball.

2 When you're happy with the consistency, start kneading, first in the bowl, then transfer the mixture onto a well-floured surface and continue to knead for 10 mins or until smooth and elastic but still soft. Butter a large bowl, then shape the dough into a ball and place in the prepared bowl. Cover and leave in a warm place for about 1 hr or until doubled in size.

3 Divide the dough into 6 balls and put them on a baking tray dusted with flour, then cover the tray with a damp tea towel. Heat a large non-stick frying pan over a high heat. Take one of the balls of dough and roll it out to form a teardrop shape that's about 21cm long and around 13cm at the widest part. When the pan is very hot, carefully lay the naan bread into it. Let it dry fry and puff up for about 3 mins, then turn over and cook on the other side for 3–4 mins until cooked through and charred in patches.

4 Heat the oven to its lowest setting and put the cooked naan bread on a baking tray. Brush with a little melted butter and cover with foil. Keep warm in the oven and layer up the cooked naans one on top of each other as you make them, brushing each one with melted butter or ghee as you go. Serve warm with curry or dips. Will keep in the freezer for up to 3 months.

Nutrition per naan (8):
Kcals 224, fat 8g, saturates 4g, carbs 31g, sugars 3g, fibre 1g, protein 6g, salt 0.4g

Chapter 2:
BREAKFAST & BRUNCH

Rather than reaching for a bowl of UPF-filled cereal or granola, start your day off right with something homemade and filled with goodness.

Homemade granola

Swap out UPF-filled granola for your own version, packed with heart-healthy oats, seeds, nuts and berries. Make sure you use vanilla extract and not essence to avoid any UPFs.

PREP 10 mins plus cooling   COOK 25 mins   15

- 2 tbsp cold pressed rapeseed oil
- 125ml maple syrup
- 2 tbsp honey
- 1 tsp vanilla extract
- 300g rolled oats
- 50g sunflower seeds
- 4 tbsp sesame seeds
- 50g pumpkin seeds
- 100g flaked almonds
- 100g dried berries
- 50g coconut flakes or desiccated coconut

1 Heat the oven to 150C/130C fan/gas 2. Mix the oil, maple syrup, honey and vanilla in a large bowl. Tip in all the remaining ingredients, except the dried fruit and coconut, and mix well.

2 Tip the granola onto two baking sheets and spread evenly. Bake for 15 mins, then mix in the coconut and dried fruit, and bake for 10–15 mins more. Remove and scrape onto a flat tray to cool. Serve with cold milk or plain yogurt. The granola can be stored in an airtight container for up to a month.

Nutrition per serving:
Kcals 259, fat 15g, saturates 3g, carbs 28g, sugars 13g, fibre 3g, protein 6g, salt 0.02g

Easy egg muffins

Make these egg muffins with the kids for breakfast or grab to go! Many breakfast cereals and options are UPFs, so making your own is an easy way to reduce your consumption.

PREP 15 mins   COOK 25 mins   4

- 1 tbsp cold pressed rapeseed oil
- 150g broccoli, finely chopped
- 1 red pepper, finely chopped
- 2 spring onions, sliced
- 6 large eggs
- 1 tbsp milk
- large pinch of smoked paprika
- 50g cheddar or gruyère, grated
- small handful of chives, chopped (optional)

1 Heat the oven to 200C/180C fan/gas 4. Brush half the oil in an 8-hole muffin tin. Heat the remaining oil in a frying pan and add the broccoli, pepper and spring onions. Fry for 5 mins. Set aside to cool.

2 Whisk the eggs with the milk, smoked paprika and half the cheese in a bowl. Add the cooked veg. Pour the egg mixture into the muffin holes and top each with the remaining cheese and a few chives, if you like. Bake for 15–17 mins or until golden brown and cooked through.

Nutrition per serving:
Kcals 229, fat 16g, saturates 5g, carbs 2g, sugars 2g, fibre 2g, protein 17g, salt 0.6g

Cinnamon & berry granola bars

You can pack these into your lunchbox for a mid-afternoon slump or grab one for breakfast on the run. Packed with goodness, they make a great alternative to any shop-bought version.

🕐 PREP 15 mins plus cooling   COOK 30 mins   ◔ Makes 12 bars

- 100g butter, plus extra for the tin
- 200g porridge oats
- 100g sunflower seeds
- 50g sesame seeds
- 50g chopped walnuts
- 3 tbsp honey
- 100g soft light brown muscovado sugar
- 1 tsp ground cinnamon
- 100g dried cranberries, cherries or blueberries, or a mix

1 Heat the oven to 160C/140C fan/gas 3. Butter and line the base of an 18 x 25cm tin. Mix the oats, seeds and nuts in a roasting tin, then put in the oven for 5–10 mins to toast.

2 Meanwhile, warm the butter, honey and sugar in a pan, stirring until the butter is melted. Add the oat mix, cinnamon and dried fruit, then mix until all the oats are well coated. Tip into the tin, press down lightly, then bake for 30 mins. Cool in the tin, then cut into 12 bars. Will keep in an airtight container for up to 5 days.

Nutrition per bar:
Kcals 294, fat 17g, saturates 6g, carbs 30g, sugars 17g, fibre 3g, protein 6g, salt 0.14g

Herb omelette with fried tomatoes

Protein-rich and on the table in 10 minutes, this omelette makes a lovely breakfast for 2. Serve with juicy, ripe fried tomatoes.

 PREP 5 mins   COOK 5 mins   2

- 1 tsp olive oil
- 3 tomatoes, halved
- 4 large eggs
- 1 tbsp chopped parsley
- 1 tbsp chopped basil

1 Heat the oil in a small non-stick frying pan, then cook the tomatoes cut-side down until starting to soften and colour. Meanwhile, beat the eggs with the herbs and plenty of freshly ground black pepper in a small bowl.

2 Scoop the tomatoes from the pan and put them on 2 serving plates. Pour the egg mixture into the pan and stir gently with a wooden spoon so the egg that sets on the base of the pan moves to enable uncooked egg to flow into the space. Stop stirring when it's nearly cooked to allow it to set into an omelette. Cut into 4 and serve with the tomatoes.

Nutrition per serving:
Kcals 204, fat 14g, saturates 4g, carbs 4g, sugars 4g, fibre 1g, protein 17g, salt 0.5g

One-pan egg & veg brunch

Great for a weekend brunch and made even easier by cooking it all in one pan, so you have less washing up to do.

PREP 5 mins   COOK 25 mins   4

- 300g baby new potatoes, halved
- ½ tbsp cold pressed rapeseed oil
- 1 knob of butter
- 1 courgette, cut into small chunks
- 1 yellow pepper, cut into small chunks
- 1 red pepper, cut into small chunks
- 2 spring onions, finely sliced
- 1 garlic clove, crushed
- 1 sprig thyme, leaves picked
- 4 eggs
- homemade toast, to serve

1 Boil the new potatoes for 8 mins, then drain. Heat the oil and butter in a large non-stick frying pan, then add the courgette, peppers, potatoes and a little salt and pepper. Cook for 10 mins, stirring from time to time until everything is starting to brown. Add the spring onions, garlic and thyme and cook for 2 mins more.

2 Make 4 spaces in the pan and crack in the eggs. Cover with foil or a lid and cook for around 4 mins, or until the eggs are cooked (with the yolks soft for dipping into). Sprinkle with more thyme leaves and ground black pepper if you like. Serve with homemade toast.

Nutrition per serving:
Kcals 170, fat 7g, saturates 2g, carbs 15g, sugars 5g, fibre 4g, protein 9g, salt 0.22g

Two-minute breakfast smoothie

This smoothie can be made in a flash, is low in fat and with no additives or thickeners, it's better for you than a shop-bought one. Use vanilla extract, not essence, to avoid any UPFs.

 PREP 2 mins 2

- 1 banana
- 1 tbsp porridge oats
- 80g soft fruit (whatever you have – strawberries, blueberries and mango all work well)
- 150ml milk
- 1 tsp honey
- 1 tsp vanilla extract

1 Put all the ingredients in a blender and whizz for 1 min until smooth.

2 Pour the banana oat smoothie into 2 glasses to serve.

Nutrition per serving:
Kcals 156, fat 3g, saturates 2g, carbs 25g, sugars 19g, fibre 2g, protein 4g, salt 0.1g

Winter breakfast hash

Filled with wintery veg like potatoes and Brussels sprouts, celebrate the colder season with this cosy hash.

PREP 15 mins   COOK 35 mins   2

- 375g potatoes, cut into small chunks
- 1 tbsp cold pressed rapeseed oil
- 1 onion (about 200g), chopped
- ½ tsp caraway seeds
- 2 garlic cloves, chopped
- 1 green pepper, deseeded and diced
- 200g large Brussels sprouts, trimmed and sliced
- 2 eggs

1 Boil the potatoes for 15 mins until tender. Meanwhile, heat the oil in a large non-stick frying pan over a medium heat and fry the onion for 8 mins, stirring frequently until it starts to colour. Add the caraway, garlic, pepper and sprouts and cook for 5 mins more with the lid on the pan so they steam at the same time.

2 Drain and lightly crush the cooked potatoes using a masher. Stir them into the vegetables and cook for 5–10 mins, turning occasionally so the mixture browns.

3 Meanwhile, poach the eggs for a few minutes for a runny yolk or until cooked to your liking. Remove from the pan using a slotted spoon. Serve each portion of hash topped with an egg.

Nutrition per serving:
Kcals 370, fat 13g, saturates 2g, carbs 42g, sugars 12g, fibre 12g, protein 15g, salt 0.2g

Feel-good muffins

Fibre-packed oats and prunes make the base of these cinnamon-spiced muffins, which are ideal for breakfast on the go. Use vanilla extract, not essence, to avoid any UPFs.

PREP 10 mins   COOK 25 mins   Makes 6–8 muffins

- 175g self-raising flour
- 50g porridge oats
- 140g light brown muscovado sugar
- 2 tsp ground cinnamon
- ½ tsp bicarbonate of soda
- 1 egg, beaten
- 150ml buttermilk
- 1 tsp vanilla extract
- 6 tbsp cold pressed sunflower oil
- 175g stoned prunes, chopped
- 85g pecans, chopped

1 Heat the oven to 200C/180C fan/gas 6. Butter 6–8 muffin tins or line them with muffin cases. Put the flour, oats, sugar, cinnamon and bicarbonate of soda in a large bowl, then rub everything through your fingers, as if making pastry, to ensure the ingredients are evenly blended.

2 Pour the egg into a jug along with the buttermilk, vanilla and oil. Lightly stir the egg mix into the flour. Fold the prunes and nuts into the mixture. Divide between the tins, filling the cases to the brim, then bake for 20–25 mins until risen and golden. Serve warm or cold. Will keep in an airtight container for up to 3 days.

Nutrition per muffin:
Kcals 478, fat 22g, saturates 2g, carbs 66g, sugars 24g, fibre 2g, protein 8g, salt 0.66g

Veggie breakfast bake

Packed with 3 of your 5 a day, get your morning off to a great start with this veggie brunch. A cracking alternative to a fry-up.

⏱ PREP 15 mins   COOK 30 mins   ◔ 4

- 4 large Portobello mushrooms
- 8 tomatoes, halved
- 1 garlic clove, thinly sliced
- 2 tsp olive oil
- 200g fresh spinach
- 4 eggs

1 Heat the oven to 200C/180C fan/gas 6. Put the mushrooms and tomatoes into an ovenproof dish. Add the garlic, drizzle over the oil and some seasoning, then bake for 10 mins.

2 Meanwhile, put the spinach into a large colander, then pour over a kettle of boiling water to wilt it. Squeeze out any excess water, then add the spinach to the dish. Make little gaps between the vegetables and crack an egg into each one. Return to the oven and cook for a further 8–10 mins or until the eggs are cooked to your liking.

Nutrition per serving:
Kcals 127, fat 8g, saturates 2g, carbs 5g, sugars 5g, fibre 3g, protein 9g, salt 0.4g

Slow-cooker breakfast beans

Put your slow cooker to work and wake up to breakfast ready. These are a great alternative to canned baked beans and are full of protein.

🕐 PREP 30 mins   COOK 5 hrs   🥧 4

- 1 tbsp olive oil
- 1 onion, thinly sliced
- 2 garlic cloves, chopped
- 1 tbsp white or red wine vinegar
- 1 heaped tbsp soft brown sugar
- 400g can pinto beans, drained and rinsed
- 200ml passata
- small bunch coriander, chopped

1 Heat the slow cooker if necessary. Heat the oil in a large frying pan and fry the onion until it starts to brown, then add the garlic and cook for 1 min. Add the vinegar and sugar and bubble for a minute. Stir in the beans and passata and season with black pepper. Tip everything into the slow cooker.

2 Cook on Low for 5 hours. If the sauce seems a little thin, turn the heat to High and cook for a few more minutes. Stir through the coriander.

Nutrition per serving:
Kcals 149, fat 3g, saturates 0.5g, carbs 21g, sugars 12g, fibre 5g, protein 6g, salt 0.39g

Breakfast pancake platter

Nutty spelt flour makes the base of these American-style weekend pancakes, You can go sweet, savoury or both! Do check labels as some soft cheeses contain additional ingredients.

 PREP 10 mins   COOK 20 mins   4

- 100g wholemeal plain spelt flour
- 2 eggs, whites and yolks separated
- 150ml semi-skimmed milk
- drop of cold pressed sunflower oil, for cooking (optional)

For the toppings
- 100g cooked salmon, broken into large flakes
- 85g low-fat soft cheese
- ¼ cucumber, sliced
- ½ lemon, cut into wedges
- 1 small red onion, thinly sliced
- 2 x 120g pots natural yogurt
- 1 banana, peeled and sliced
- 160g mixed berries (we used blueberries, raspberries and cherries)
- capers, dill and sliced spring onions, walnuts, mixed seeds, ground cinnamon and maple syrup, to serve (optional)

1 Tip the flour into a bowl, then whisk in the egg yolks and half the milk until smooth. Slowly whisk in the rest of the milk (the batter will be runny). Whisk the egg whites to soft peaks in a separate bowl, then gently fold this into the batter.

2 Heat a large non-stick pan over a medium heat and wipe a drop of oil around the base using a kitchen towel. Spoon in 2 tbsp of batter per pancake (you should be able to make 3 at a time, well-spaced apart) and cook for about 2–3 mins until bubbles appear on the surface and the bottom is set. Flip using a palette knife and cook for another 2–3 mins.

3 Arrange the pancakes in a single layer over a large serving platter, then top one side with the salmon, soft cheese, cucumber slices, lemon wedges and onion slices. Top the other side with the yogurt, banana slices and berries. If you like, scatter the savoury pancakes with the capers, dill and spring onions, if using, and top the sweet pancakes with walnuts, seeds, cinnamon and maple syrup. Or, serve these on the side for everyone to help themselves.

Nutrition per serving:
Kcals 371, fat 16g, saturates 5g, carbs 32g, sugars 16g, fibre 6g, protein 22g, salt 0.5g

Avocado & black bean eggs

Easy and quick to bring together for a hearty, protein-packed breakfast for two. Be sure to check the ingredients label for the beans to ensure they include just beans and water.

 PREP 5 mins   COOK 5 mins   2

- 2 tsp cold pressed rapeseed oil
- 1 red chilli, deseeded and thinly sliced
- 1 large garlic clove, sliced
- 2 large eggs
- 400g can black beans
- ½ x 400g can cherry tomatoes
- ¼ tsp cumin seeds
- 1 small avocado, halved and sliced
- handful chopped coriander
- 1 lime, cut into wedges

1 Heat the oil in a large non-stick frying pan. Add the chilli and garlic and cook until softened and starting to colour. Break in the eggs on either side of the pan. Once they start to set, spoon the beans (with their juice) and the tomatoes around the pan and sprinkle over the cumin seeds. You're aiming to warm the beans and tomatoes rather than cook them.

2 Remove the pan from the heat and scatter over the avocado and coriander. Squeeze over half of the lime wedges. Serve with the remaining wedges on the side for squeezing over.

Nutrition per serving:
Kcals 356, fat 20g, saturates 4g, carbs 18g, sugars 5g, fibre 11g, protein 20g, salt 0.8g

Chapter 3:
SOUPS

Hearty, nourishing and better for you than soup from a can. Why not make a big batch to freeze?

Roasted tomato & red pepper soup

Topped off with a spoonful of creamy ricotta and crunchy seeds, this soup may be low in calories but it's filled with flavour.

PREP 10 mins   COOK 30 mins   2

- 400g tomatoes, halved
- 1 red onion, quartered
- 2 Romano peppers, roughly chopped
- 2 tbsp olive oil
- 2 garlic cloves, bashed in their skins
- few thyme sprigs
- 1 tbsp red wine vinegar
- 2 tbsp ricotta
- few basil leaves
- 1 tbsp mixed seeds, toasted
- homemade bread, to serve

1 Heat the oven to 200C/180C fan/gas 6. Put the tomatoes, onion and peppers in a roasting tin, toss with the oil and season. Nestle in the garlic and thyme sprigs, then roast for 25–30 mins until all the veg has softened and slightly caramelised. Squeeze the garlic cloves out of their skins into the tin, strip the leaves off the thyme and discard the stalks and garlic skins. Mix the vinegar into the tin, then blend everything in a bullet blender or using a stick blender, adding enough water to loosen to your preferred consistency (we used around 150ml).

2 Reheat the soup if necessary, taste for seasoning, then spoon into 2 bowls and top each with a spoonful of ricotta, a few basil leaves, the seeds and a drizzle of oil. Serve with homemade bread for dunking.

Nutrition per serving:
Kcals 306, fat 19g, saturates 4g, carbs 22g, sugars 18g, fibre 9g, protein 8g, salt 0.1g

Green pesto minestrone

This minestrone is bright, zingy and full of goodness. If you're not using the stock recipe on page 8, remember to check the ingredients on the stock packaging.

PREP 10 mins   COOK 25 mins   4

- 2 tbsp olive oil
- 1 large onion,
  finely chopped
- 2 celery sticks,
  finely chopped
- 1.4l fresh vegetable stock
- 2 small lemons, zested
  and juiced
- 170g orzo
- 120g frozen peas
- 250g frozen spinach
- 50g fresh pesto
- 60g parmesan (or
  vegetarian alternative),
  grated
- homemade bread or
  flatbreads, to serve
  (optional)

1   Heat the oil in a large saucepan, add the onion, celery and a pinch of salt and fry for 8 mins until soft. Add the stock with the zest and juice of the lemons, and season. Stir in the orzo and cook for 5 mins, then add the peas and spinach and cook for a further 5 mins. Swirl though the pesto and season.

2   Ladle the soup generously into bowls and top with a handful of parmesan. Serve with homemade bread or flatbreads, if using, to dip. Will keep in the fridge for up to 2 days.

Nutrition per serving:
Kcals 334, fat 17g, saturates 5g, carbs 24g, sugars 9g, fibre 8g, protein 19g, salt 1.4g

Rustic vegetable soup

This vegetarian soup is packed with veggies and lentils - it's healthy, low fat and full of flavour. If you're not using the stock on page 8, check the ingredients on the stock packaging.

PREP 15 mins   COOK 30 mins   4

- 1 tbsp cold pressed rapeseed oil
- 1 large onion, chopped
- 2 carrots, chopped
- 2 celery sticks, chopped
- 50g dried red lentils
- 1.5l fresh vegetable stock, hot
- 2 tbsp tomato purée
- 1 tbsp chopped thyme
- 1 leek, finely sliced
- 175g cauliflower florets, cut into bite-sized pieces
- 1 courgette, chopped
- 3 garlic cloves, finely chopped
- ½ large Savoy cabbage, stalks removed and leaves chopped
- 1 tbsp chopped basil

1 Heat the oil in a large pan with a lid. Add the onion, carrots and celery and fry for 10 mins, stirring from time to time until they are starting to colour a little around the edges. Stir in the lentils and cook for 1 min more.

2 Pour in the hot stock, add the tomato purée and thyme and stir well. Add the leek, cauliflower, courgette and garlic, bring to the boil, then cover and leave to simmer for 15 mins.

3 Add the cabbage and basil and cook for 5 mins more until the veg is just tender. Season with pepper, ladle into bowls and serve. Will keep in the fridge for up to 3 days or in the freezer for up to 3 months.

Nutrition per serving:
Kcals 162, fat 5g, saturates 1g, carbs 19g, sugars 9g, fibre 7g, protein 7g, salt 0.4g

Celeriac soup with toasted hazelnut crumble

Serve this hearty celeriac soup for lunch or as a starter. If not using the stock recipe on page 8 or homemade breadcrumbs, check the ingredients on the stock and panko packaging.

 PREP 10 mins COOK 40 mins   4

- 1 tbsp olive oil
- 1 onion, sliced
- 2 celery sticks, diced
- 2 garlic cloves, sliced
- 1 small celeriac (about 800g), peeled and diced
- 500ml fresh vegetable stock
- ¼ tsp ground nutmeg
- 50ml low-fat crème fraîche

For the hazelnut crumble
- 2 tbsp hazelnuts, roughly chopped
- 2 tbsp panko or coarse dried breadcrumbs
- small handful finely chopped chives

1 Heat half the oil in a large saucepan over a medium-low heat. Sweat the onion, celery and garlic with the pan partially covered by the lid for 15 mins, until softened. Tip in the celeriac and pour over the stock. Bring to a simmer, cover, and cook for 15–20 mins, until the celeriac is tender. Remove from the heat, stir in the nutmeg, crème fraîche and some salt and pepper and blitz with a hand blender until smooth.

2 Meanwhile, heat the remaining oil in a frying pan over a medium heat. Fry the hazelnuts and breadcrumbs gently for a few minutes, until toasted. Put in a bowl, stir in the chives and season. Ladle the soup into bowls and spoon over the hazelnut crumble to serve.

Nutrition per serving:
Kcals 198, fat 11g, saturates 2g, carbs 14g, sugars 7g, fibre 11g, protein 5g, salt 0.9g

Mexican street corn soup

Serve up a bowl of this spicy Mexican soup for lunch or supper. If you're not using the stock recipe on page 8, remember to check the ingredients on the stock packaging.

PREP 15 mins   COOK 15 mins   4

- 1 tbsp cold pressed rapeseed oil
- 3 x 198g cans sweetcorn, drained
- 1 small onion, chopped
- 1 large potato, peeled and cut into 1cm cubes
- 1 tsp smoked paprika, plus extra to serve
- ½ tsp ground cumin
- 900ml fresh vegetable stock
- 1 lime, ½ juiced, ½ thinly sliced
- 1 green chilli, thinly sliced
- 60g feta, crumbled

1 Heat half the oil in a wide, deep saucepan over a medium–high heat. Tip in the sweetcorn, keeping it in a single layer as much as possible. Cook undisturbed for 2 mins so the kernels turn golden on the bottom. Stir, spread out again and repeat until the sweetcorn is golden and charred in spots. Cook for another 1 min, stirring, then tip everything into a large bowl.

2 Add the remaining oil to the pan and fry the onion and potato for 3–4 mins until slightly softened and pale golden. Add the spices and cook for a further minute, then pour in the stock. Spoon 3 tbsp of the sweetcorn into a small bowl, then add the rest to the pan. Bring to the boil, then reduce the heat to a simmer, cover and cook for 5–10 mins, or until the potato is fully softened.

3 Remove the pan from the heat and squeeze in the lime juice. Blitz using a hand blender (or tip into a blender to do this) until smooth and creamy. Season to taste. Divide the soup between 4 bowls and top with the reserved sweetcorn, the chilli, lime slices, feta and a sprinkle of paprika.

Nutrition per serving:
Kcals 236, fat 9g, saturates 3g, carbs 29g, sugars 12g, fibre 7g, protein 7g, salt 1g

Carrot & lentil soup with feta

Lentils are rich in protein, fibre, iron and B vitamins. Pack in a thermos for a UPF-free lunch to go. If you're not using the stock on page 8, check the ingredients on the stock packaging.

PREP 20 mins   COOK 35 mins   6

- 2 tbsp cold pressed rapeseed oil
- 3 onions (420g), chopped
- 5 garlic cloves, chopped
- 750g carrots, sliced
- 1 tbsp smoked paprika
- 1 tbsp ground coriander
- 1 tbsp thyme leaves
- 300g red lentils
- 1.3l fresh vegetable stock, hot
- 2 x 400g cans chickpeas
- 150g feta, crumbled

1 Heat the oil in a large pan over a medium heat and fry the onions for 10 mins, stirring frequently until starting to turn golden. Add the garlic and carrots, and cook a few minutes more, then stir in the spices, thyme and lentils.

2 Pour in the stock, then cover and simmer for 20 mins until the lentils are pulpy and tender. Remove from the heat and roughly blitz using a hand blender – you don't want it to be completely smooth. Stir in the chickpeas and the liquid from the cans and reheat the soup. Serve with the feta scattered over the top. Will keep in the fridge for up to 4 days or in the freezer for up to 3 months.

Nutrition per serving:
Kcals 462, fat 13g, saturates 4g, carbs 54g, sugars 14g, fibre 14g, protein 24g, salt 1.27g

Italian vegetable soup

Cook and freeze this soup for when you're low on time, so you're not reaching for a ready meal. If you're not using the stock on page 8, check the ingredients on the stock packaging.

PREP 15 mins   COOK 55 mins   8

- 2 onions, finely chopped
- 2 carrots, roughly chopped
- 4 celery sticks,
  roughly chopped
- 1 tbsp olive oil
- 2 tbsp sugar
- 4 garlic cloves, crushed
- 2 tbsp tomato purée
- 2 bay leaves
- few thyme sprigs
- 3 courgettes,
  roughly chopped
- 400g can butter
  beans, drained
- 400g can chopped
  tomatoes
- 1.2l vegetable stock
- 100g parmesan (or
  vegetarian equivalent),
  grated
- 140g small pasta shapes
- Small bunch basil,
  roughly chopped

1 Gently cook the onion, carrot and celery in the oil in a large saucepan for 20 mins, until soft. Splash in water if they stick. Add the sugar, garlic, tomato purée, herbs and courgettes and cook for 4–5 mins on a medium heat until they brown a little.

2 Pour in the beans, tomatoes and stock, then simmer for 20 mins. If you're freezing it, cool and do so now, if not, add half the parmesan and the pasta and simmer for 6–8 mins until the pasta is cooked. Sprinkle with basil and the remaining parmesan to serve. If freezing, defrost then reheat before adding the pasta and cheese and continuing as above. This soup will keep in the freezer for up to 3 months.

Nutrition per serving:
Kcals 215, fat 6g, saturates 3g, carbs 30g, sugars 12g, fibre 5g, protein 11g, salt 1.06g

Spicy roasted parsnip soup

This aromatic soup is perfect for an autumnal day. If not using the stock recipe on page 8, remember to check the ingredients on the stock packaging.

PREP 10 mins   COOK 35 mins   4

- 2 tbsp olive oil
- 1 tsp coriander seeds
- 1 tsp cumin seeds, plus extra to garnish
- ½ tsp ground turmeric
- ½ tsp mustard seeds
- 1 large onion, cut into 8 chunks
- 2 garlic cloves
- 675g parsnips, diced
- 2 plum tomatoes, quartered
- 1.2l fresh vegetable stock
- 1 tbsp lemon juice

1 Heat the oven to 220C/200C fan/gas 7. In a bowl, mix together the olive oil, coriander, cumin, turmeric and mustard seeds. Add the onion, garlic, parsnips and tomatoes, then mix well. Spread over a large, heavy baking sheet, then roast for 30 mins until tender.

2 Spoon into a food processor or liquidiser with 600ml of the vegetable stock and blitz until smooth. Pour into a pan with the remaining vegetable stock, season, then heat until barely simmering. Remove from the heat and stir in the lemon juice. Garnish with cumin seeds.

Nutrition per serving:
Kcals 233, fat 10g, saturates 1g, carbs 30g, sugars 0g, fibre 10g, protein 6g, salt 1.1g

Roasted roots & sage soup

Wintery root veg are the star of this soup, complemented by earthy sage. If not using the stock recipe on page 8, remember to check the ingredients on the stock packaging.

PREP 15 mins   COOK 45 mins   2

- 1 parsnip, chopped
- 2 carrots, chopped
- 300g turnip, swede or celeriac, chopped
- 4 garlic cloves, skin left on
- 1 tbsp cold pressed rapeseed oil, plus ½ tsp
- 1 tsp maple syrup
- ¼ small bunch sage, leaves picked, 4 whole, the rest finely chopped
- 750ml fresh vegetable stock
- grating of nutmeg
- 1½ tbsp fat-free natural yogurt

1 Heat the oven to 200C/180C fan/gas 6. Toss the root vegetables and garlic with the oil and season. Tip onto a baking tray and roast for 30 mins until tender. Toss with the maple syrup and the chopped sage, then roast for another 10 mins until golden and glazed. Brush the whole sage leaves with ½ tsp oil and add to the baking tray in the last 3–4 mins to crisp up, then remove and set aside.

2 Scrape the vegetables into a pan, squeeze the garlic out of the skins, discarding the papery shells, and add with the stock, then blend with a stick blender until very smooth and creamy. Bring to a simmer and season with salt, pepper and nutmeg.

3 Divide between bowls. Serve with a swirl of yogurt and the crispy sage leaves.

Nutrition per serving:
Kcals 221, fat 9g, saturates 1g, carbs 26g, sugars 18g, fibre 10g, protein 5g, salt 0.2g

Indian winter soup

Make the most of your spice rack with this spice-filled soup. It is high in fibre, low in fat and can be frozen for ultimate convenience.

PREP 15 mins   COOK 30 mins   4–6

- 100g pearl barley
- 2 tbsp cold pressed rapeseed oil
- ½ tsp brown mustard seeds
- 1 tsp cumin seeds
- 2 green chillies, deseeded and finely chopped
- 1 bay leaf
- 2 cloves
- 1 small cinnamon stick
- ½ tsp ground turmeric
- 1 large onion, chopped
- 2 garlic cloves, finely chopped
- 1 parsnip, cut into chunks
- 200g butternut squash, cut into chunks
- 200g sweet potato, cut into chunks
- 1 tsp paprika
- 1 tsp ground coriander
- 225g red lentils
- 2 tomatoes, chopped
- small bunch coriander, chopped
- 1 tsp grated ginger
- 1 tsp lemon juice

1 Rinse the pearl barley and cook following the pack instructions. When it is tender, drain and set aside. Meanwhile, heat the oil in a deep, heavy-bottomed pan. Fry the mustard seeds, cumin seeds, chillies, bay leaf, cloves, cinnamon and turmeric until fragrant and the seeds start to crackle. Tip in the onion and garlic, then cook for 5–8 mins until soft. Stir in the parsnip, butternut and sweet potato and mix thoroughly, making sure the vegetables are fully coated with the oil and spices. Sprinkle in the paprika, ground coriander and seasoning, and stir again.

2 Add the lentils, pearl barley, tomatoes and 1.7 litres water. Bring to the boil, then turn down and simmer until the vegetables are tender. When the lentils are almost cooked, stir in the chopped coriander, ginger and lemon juice. Store in the freezer for up to 3 months.

Nutrition per serving (4):
Kcals 445, fat 8g, saturates 1g, carbs 80g, sugars 13g, fibre 8g, protein 19g, salt 0.14g

Mushroom soup

Make the most of mushrooms with this soup made from cream, onions and garlic. If not using one of the stock recipes on pages 8 and 9, check the ingredients on the stock packaging.

PREP 10 mins   COOK 25 mins   4

- 90g butter
- 2 onions, roughly chopped
- 1 garlic clove, crushed
- 500g mushrooms, finely chopped (chestnut or button mushrooms work well)
- 2 tbsp plain flour
- 1l fresh chicken or vegetable stock
- 1 bay leaf
- 4 tbsp single cream
- small handful flat-leaf parsley, roughly chopped, to serve (optional)

1 Heat the butter in a large saucepan and cook the onions and garlic until soft but not browned, about 8–10 mins. Add the mushrooms and cook over a high heat for another 3 mins until softened. Sprinkle over the flour and stir to combine. Pour in the chicken stock, bring the mixture to the boil, then add the bay leaf and simmer for another 10 mins.

2 Remove and discard the bay leaf, then remove the mushroom mixture from the heat and blitz using a hand blender until smooth. Gently reheat the soup and stir through the cream (or, you could freeze the soup at this stage – simply stir through the cream when heating). Scatter over the parsley, if you like, and serve. Will keep frozen for up to 3 months.

Nutrition per serving:
Kcals 309, fat 22g, saturates 14g, carbs 14g, sugars 5g, fibre 3g, protein 11g, salt 1.8g

Spiced lentil & butternut squash soup

Cook a batch of this and freeze the leftovers for a speedy supper another day. It's healthy and low in fat too. If not using the stock on page 8, check the ingredients on the stock packaging.

 PREP 10 mins   COOK 40 mins   4–6

- 2 tbsp olive oil
- 2 onions, finely chopped
- 2 garlic cloves, crushed
- ¼ tsp hot chilli powder
- 1 tbsp ras el hanout
- 1 butternut squash, peeled and cut into 2cm pieces
- 100g red lentils
- 1l fresh vegetable stock, hot
- small bunch coriander, leaves chopped, plus extra to serve

To serve
- dukkah and natural yogurt

1 Heat the oil in a large flameproof casserole dish or saucepan over a medium–high heat. Fry the onions with a pinch of salt for 7 mins, or until softened and just caramelised. Add the garlic, chilli and ras el hanout, and cook for 1 min more.

2 Stir in the squash and lentils. Pour over the stock and season to taste. Bring to the boil, then reduce the heat to a simmer and cook, covered, for 25 mins or until the squash is soft. Blitz the soup with a hand blender until smooth, then season to taste.

3 Stir in the coriander leaves and ladle the soup into bowls. Serve topped with the dukkah, yogurt and extra coriander leaves. Will keep in the fridge for up to 3 days or in the freezer for up to 3 months.

Nutrition per serving (6):
Kcals 167, fat 5g, saturates 1g, carbs 23g, sugars 4g, fibre 3g, protein 6g, salt 0.5g

Chapter 4:
LIGHT LUNCHES & LUNCHBOXES

Head to the fridge instead of the shops for your lunch so you can enjoy a delicious UPF-free lunch that is healthy and filling.

Brown rice tabbouleh with eggs & parsley

Pack up this tasty rice salad for a healthy vegetarian lunch. It's full of fibre, folate and vitamin C and is topped with protein-rich boiled eggs.

 PREP 10 mins   COOK 20 mins   2

- 75g brown basmati rice
- thyme sprig
- 160g celery sticks, chopped
- 2 large eggs
- 1 small lemon, zested and juiced
- 1 small red onion, finely chopped
- 3 tbsp parsley, chopped
- ½ pomegranate, seeds only

1 Simmer the rice with the thyme and celery for 20 mins until tender. Meanwhile, boil the eggs for 7 mins, then cool in cold water and carefully peel off the shell.

2 Drain the rice and tip into a bowl. Add the lemon zest and juice and the onion and season well. Stir to combine, then scatter over the parsley and pomegranate. Spoon onto plates or into lunchboxes, then halve or quarter the eggs and arrange on top.

Nutrition per serving:
Kcals 294, fat 8g, saturates 2g, carbs 37g, sugars 9g, fibre 6g, protein 15g, salt 0.38g

Chicken, mango & noodle salad

Ditch the pre-packaged sandwiches and stir this together for your lunchbox the night before. It uses leftover chicken, so is perfect the day after a Sunday roast.

 PREP 15 mins 4

- 200g vermicelli rice noodles
- 2 limes, juiced, plus wedges to serve (optional)
- 1 tbsp fish sauce
- 1 tbsp honey, plus 1 tsp
- 1 tbsp toasted sesame oil
- 320g leftover cooked chicken, shredded
- 2 ripe mangoes, stoned, peeled and cut into thin slices
- 20g coriander, roughly chopped
- 2 red chillies, seeds removed and thinly sliced

1 Put the noodles in a heatproof bowl, cover with boiling water and leave for 15 mins to soften. Meanwhile, combine the lime juice, fish sauce, honey and sesame oil in a small bowl and whisk together.

2 Drain and rinse the noodles briefly under cold water. Drain again and tip into a large bowl along with the remaining ingredients, except the lime wedges. Pour over the dressing and toss together with seasoning to taste. Divide among 4 plates and serve with the lime wedges on the side, if you like.

Nutrition per serving:
Kcals 424, fat 9g, saturates 2g, carbs 56g, sugars 17g, fibre 4g, protein 27g, salt 1.2g

Butternut biryani with cucumber raita

Containing 3 of your 5-a-day along with calcium, iron and fibre, this veggie biryani is served with a creamy raita, making it an ideal filling lunch that's quick to put together.

🕐 PREP 15 mins   COOK 30 mins   🥧 2

- 20g dried porcini mushrooms, roughly chopped
- 1 tbsp cold pressed rapeseed oil
- 2 onions, sliced
- 2 garlic cloves, crushed
- 1 tbsp chopped fresh ginger
- 1 red chilli, deseeded and chopped
- 85g brown basmati rice
- 160g diced butternut squash (prepared weight)
- 1 tsp cumin seeds
- 1 tsp ground coriander
- 10cm length cucumber, grated, core removed
- 125g natural yogurt
- 2 tbsp chopped mint, plus a few leaves
- ⅓ pack coriander, chopped
- 25g toasted flaked almonds

1 Pour 425ml boiling water over the dried mushrooms and set aside.

2 Heat the oil in a non-stick pan. Add the onions, garlic, ginger and chilli and stir-fry briefly over a high heat so they start to soften. Add the rice and squash and stir for a few minutes. Tip in the cumin and coriander, then stir in the mushrooms and their water and season well.

3 Cover the pan and simmer for 20 mins until the rice is tender. Meanwhile, mix the cucumber and yogurt with the mint to make a raita. Stir the coriander and almonds into the rice when it is ready and serve with the raita and a few extra leaves of mint or coriander.

Nutrition per serving:
Kcals 463, fat 17g, saturates 2g, carbs 58g, sugars 15g, fibre 7g, protein 16g, salt 0.17g

Soy & butter salmon parcels

These salmon parcels are served with a refreshing cucumber and sesame salad on the side and are simple to make. A light and quick weekend lunch.

 PREP 20 mins   COOK 10 mins   4

- 2 tbsp butter
- 4 x 100g skinless salmon fillets
- 2 tbsp low-salt soy sauce
- 1 tbsp honey
- 1 tbsp sesame seeds
- 2 spring onions, sliced
- 1 cucumber, finely sliced
- few drops sesame oil

1 Heat a griddle pan on a medium–high heat. Cut 4 pieces of foil that will easily wrap a piece of salmon and lay them on the work surface. Spread a little butter onto the centre of each piece of foil to stop the salmon sticking. Lay the salmon on top. Mix the soy with the honey and divide it among the parcels, pouring it over the salmon. Dot any remaining butter on top and then fold the foil around the salmon tightly to make a parcel.

2 Put the parcels on the griddle and cook for 5–10 mins. Check a parcel to see how it's getting along but be careful – it will be hot. Once the salmon is cooked, open the parcels and scatter some sesame seeds and spring onion into each.

3 Meanwhile, mix the cucumber with a few drops of sesame oil and season with a little salt. Serve the salmon with the cucumber salad and some rice, if you like.

Nutrition per serving:
Kcals 307, fat 22g, saturates 7g, carbs 5g, sugars 5g, fibre 1g, protein 21g, salt 1.1g

Minty beetroot, feta & bulgur salad

This salad is made in just 10 minutes, making it a perfect packed lunch. It looks just as good as it tastes, with vibrant oranges, beetroot and mint.

PREP 5 mins   COOK 5 mins   2

- 50g bulgur wheat
- 2 oranges, ½ zested and juiced, the rest peeled and chopped
- 1 garlic clove, finely chopped
- 1 tsp apple cider vinegar
- 3 tbsp chopped mint
- 3 spring onions, sliced
- 4 walnut halves, broken
- 4 pitted Kalamata olives, halved (optional)
- 2 cooked beetroots, chopped
- 40g feta

1 Put the bulgur in a small pan, cover with water, bring to the boil, then cook, covered, for 5 mins or until tender. Drain well, press out any excess water and tip into a bowl.

2 Stir in the orange zest and juice, garlic and vinegar, then toss through the mint, spring onions, walnuts and olives (if using). Finally, stir in the chopped beetroot and orange, spoon into containers and top with the feta to mix through just before eating.

Nutrition per serving:
Kcals 270, fat 10g, saturates 3g, carbs 31g, sugars 16g, fibre 8g, protein 11g, salt 0.7g

Spicy chickpea stew

Filled with plant-based protein from the chickpeas, which also pack in lots of fibre, this spicy stew is great for gut health and easy to reheat.

 PREP 20 mins   COOK 45 mins   4

- 1 tbsp cold pressed rapeseed oil
- 2 onions, roughly chopped
- 2 green peppers, deseeded and cut into cubes
- 2 tsp hot chilli powder
- 1 tbsp ground coriander
- 1 tsp ground cumin
- 500ml carton passata
- 2 x 400g cans chickpeas
- 40g flame raisins
- ½ lemon, juiced, flesh scooped out and white pith removed, then zest finely chopped (you'll need 2 tsp)
- 350g cauliflower florets
- 15g parsley, chopped
- 140g wholemeal couscous
- 40g toasted flaked almonds

1 Heat the oil in a large lidded pan over a medium heat and fry the onions for 10 mins, stirring often until golden. Stir in the peppers and cook for 5 mins more.

2 Add the chilli powder, coriander and cumin, stir briefly, then tip in the passata and chickpeas along with the liquid from the cans.

3 Stir in the raisins and lemon zest and some seasoning, then add the cauliflower. Cover tightly and simmer over a medium heat for 15–20 mins until the cauliflower is tender. Stir in half the parsley.

4 Meanwhile, put the couscous in a heatproof bowl and pour over 175ml boiling water from the kettle. Stir in the lemon juice, then cover and let stand for about 10 mins until the couscous has absorbed the liquid and is tender. Stir in the toasted flaked almonds and most of the remaining parsley.

5 Divide half the couscous between 2 plates and top with half the chickpea stew and the rest of the parsley. Leave the remainder to cool for another day. Will keep covered and chilled for up to 3 days. Reheat the stew in a pan over a low heat with a splash of water until piping hot. Reheat the couscous in the microwave.

Nutrition per serving:
Kcals 509, fat 15g, saturates 2g, carbs 62g, sugars 22g, fibre 20g, protein 22g, salt 0.37g

Chicken, broccoli & beetroot salad with avocado pesto

Packed with hearty superfoods like nigella seeds, walnuts, avocado oil and red onion to give your body a boost.

 PREP 15 mins   COOK 15 mins   4

- 250g thin-stemmed broccoli
- 2 tsp avocado oil
- 3 skinless chicken breasts
- 1 red onion, thinly sliced
- 100g bag watercress
- 2 raw beetroots (about 175g), peeled and julienned or grated
- 1 tsp nigella seeds

For the avocado pesto
- small pack basil
- 1 avocado
- ½ garlic clove, crushed
- 25g walnut halves, crumbled
- 1 tbsp avocado oil
- 1 lemon, zested and juiced

1 Bring a large pan of water to the boil, add the broccoli and cook for 2 mins. Drain, then refresh under cold water. Heat a griddle pan, toss the broccoli in ½ tsp of the oil and griddle for 2–3 mins, turning, until a little charred. Set aside to cool. Brush the chicken with the remaining oil and season. Griddle for 3–4 mins each side or until cooked through. Leave to cool, then slice or shred into chunky pieces.

2 Next, make the pesto. Pick the leaves from the basil and set aside a handful to top the salad. Put the rest in the small bowl of a food processor. Scoop the flesh from the avocado and add to the food processor with the garlic, walnuts, oil, 1 tbsp lemon juice, 2–3 tbsp cold water and some seasoning. Blitz until smooth, then transfer to a small serving dish. Pour the remaining lemon juice over the sliced onions and leave for a few minutes.

3 Pile the watercress onto a large platter. Toss through the broccoli and onion, along with the lemon juice they were soaked in. Top with the beetroot, but don't mix it in, and the chicken. Scatter over the reserved basil leaves, the lemon zest and nigella seeds, then serve with the avocado pesto.

Nutrition per serving:
Kcals 320, fat 18g, saturates 3g, carbs 8g, sugars 6g, fibre 6g, protein 29g, salt 0.3g

Burrito bowl with chipotle black beans

This healthy burrito bowl is chock full of veggies and greens, perfect for a filling lunch. Check the label on the beans to make sure there are only beans and water listed in the ingredients.

 PREP 15 mins   COOK 15 mins   2

- 125g basmati rice
- 1 tbsp olive oil
- 2 garlic cloves, chopped
- 400g can black beans, drained and rinsed
- 1 tbsp apple cider vinegar
- 1 tsp honey
- 1 tbsp chipotle paste
- 100g chopped curly kale
- 1 avocado, halved and sliced
- 1 tomato, chopped
- 1 small red onion, chopped

To serve (optional)
- chipotle hot sauce
- coriander leaves
- lime wedges

1 Cook the rice following the pack instructions, then drain and return to the pan to keep warm. In a frying pan, heat the oil, add the garlic and fry for 2 mins or until golden. Add the beans, vinegar, honey and chipotle. Season and warm through for 2 mins.

2 Boil the kale for 1 min, then drain, squeezing out any excess water. Divide the rice between big, shallow bowls and top with the beans, kale, avocado, tomato and onion. Serve with hot sauce, coriander and lime wedges, if you like.

Nutrition per serving:
Kcals 573, fat 21g, saturates 4g, carbs 72g, sugars 7g, fibre 15g, protein 16g, salt 0.8g

Sesame chicken noodles

Forget soggy lunchbox sandwiches and whip up a tasty and healthy chicken and noodle salad for lunch using leftover cooked chicken.

PREP 10 mins plus cooling   COOK 45 mins   2

- 1 aubergine
- 2 garlic cloves, skin on
- 1 tbsp olive oil
- 1 tbsp tahini
- 1 lime, juiced
- 2 tsp soy sauce
- 1 tsp sesame oil
- ½ tsp chilli flakes, plus extra to serve
- 200g cooked rice noodles
- 200g leftover cooked chicken
- 1 carrot, grated
- ½ cucumber, seeds removed and cut into half moons
- ½ small pack mint, roughly chopped

1 Heat the oven to 200C/180C fan/gas 6. Pierce the aubergine a few times with the tip of a knife, then toss with the garlic and olive oil and put on a baking sheet. Roast for about 40–45 mins, or until the aubergine is completely tender. Set aside to cool, then roughly chop the aubergine.

2 Tip the tahini, lime juice, soy sauce, sesame oil and chilli flakes into a large bowl, then squeeze out the roasted garlic from their papery skins. Whisk in enough water to make a creamy dressing.

3 Add the noodles, leftover chicken, aubergine and carrot and toss everything to combine, then gently fold through the cucumber and mint. Divide between 2 containers, then sprinkle over a few extra chilli flakes to serve.

Nutrition per serving:
Kcals 517, fat 26g, saturates 5g, carbs 33g, sugars 8g, fibre 9g, protein 33g, salt 0.99g

Veggie hummus pasta salad

This includes homemade hummus and any extra can be refrigerated if you want to make a smaller portion of salad. For a variation, scatter with pil biber chilli flakes and crumbled feta.

PREP 20 mins   COOK 10 mins   4

- 400g can chickpeas, drained and liquid reserved
- 1 tbsp tahini
- 2 tbsp extra virgin olive oil
- ½ garlic clove
- ½ lemon, zested and juiced
- 250g short pasta of your choice
- 50g baby spinach, roughly chopped
- 200g cherry tomatoes halved (we used a mixture of red and yellow)
- ¼ cucumber, quartered lengthways and cut into small triangles
- 75g pitted olives of your choice, roughly chopped

1 Boil the kettle. Tip half the chickpeas into a food processor, add roughly half the reserved liquid from the can (the liquid should come to just below the level of the chickpeas in the blender), the tahini, olive oil, garlic, lemon zest and juice and some seasoning. Blitz until you have a smooth, loose hummus. Check for seasoning.

2 Cook the pasta following the pack instructions. Drain, reserving a mugful of the cooking water, and rinse the pasta under cold running water for a few seconds until cool.

3 Toss the cooked pasta, spinach, tomatoes, cucumbers, olives, the rest of the chickpeas and the hummus dressing together in a large bowl until everything is well-coated. Add a splash of the reserved pasta cooking water if the dressing is too thick. Will keep covered and chilled for up to 6 hrs or in an airtight container in a cool bag for 2 hrs. Add a splash of water to loosen the dressing again before serving.

Nutrition per serving:
Kcals 385, fat 12g, saturates 2g, carbs 51g, sugars 3g, fibre 9g, protein 13g, salt 0.7g

Lentil & tuna salad

Throw together this no-cook lentil and tuna salad for a healthy lunch. It takes just 15 minutes to make – ideal for busy days. The salad can be cut down for individual lunchbox portions.

 PREP 15 mins 4

- 2 tbsp sherry vinegar
- 1 tsp Dijon mustard
- 2 garlic cloves, finely grated
- 50ml olive oil
- 2 x 250g pouches ready-cooked puy lentils
- 2 x 160g cans tuna steaks in spring water, drained and flaked
- 160g cherry tomatoes, halved (about 10)
- 2 ready-roasted peppers, chopped
- handful parsley, finely chopped
- ½ small bunch chives, finely chopped, plus extra to garnish

1 Whisk the vinegar, mustard and garlic together in a small bowl. Slowly drizzle in the oil, whisking as you go, until emulsified, then season to taste.

2 Add the lentils, tuna, tomatoes, peppers and herbs to a large bowl and toss together. Pour over the dressing and toss again. Divide among 4 bowls and garnish with the remaining chives.

Nutrition per serving:
Kcals 374, fat 15g, saturates 2g, carbs 26g, sugars 3g, fibre 9g, protein 28g, salt 0.7g

Pineapple fried rice

This fresh pineapple fried rice works just as well as the star of the show as it does as part of a lunch spread. The rice can easily be cut down to make individual lunchbox portions.

PREP 10 mins   COOK 10 mins   4

- 1½ tbsp cold pressed rapeseed oil
- 2 eggs, beaten
- 2 garlic cloves, crushed
- small bunch spring onions, chopped
- ½ tsp Chinese five-spice powder
- 400g cooked long-grain rice
- 85g frozen peas
- 2 tsp sesame oil
- 2 tbsp low-salt soy sauce
- 400g fresh pineapple, roughly chopped into chunks (about ½ medium pineapple)

1 Heat 1 tbsp oil in a wok. Add the eggs, swirling them up the sides, to make a thin omelette. Once cooked through, roll the omelette onto a chopping board and cut into ribbons.

2 Heat the remaining oil. Add the garlic, spring onions and five-spice. Stir-fry until sizzling, then add the rice (if using pouches, squeeze them first to separate the grains), peas, sesame oil and soy. Cook over a high heat until the rice is hot, then stir through the pineapple and omelette ribbons.

Nutrition per serving:
Kcals 301, fat 9g, saturates 2g, carbs 44g, sugars 13g, fibre 4g, protein 9g, salt 0.8g

Chapter 5:
WEEKNIGHT MEALS

Familiar favourites fill this chapter, like our chicken stir-fry and chicken katsu curry, which are great for whipping up midweek.

Healthy chicken katsu curry

This healthier katsu is coated in finely chopped flaked almonds and baked in the oven (rather than fried) until crisp and golden for a less messy and quicker weeknight meal.

PREP 20 mins   COOK 35 mins   2

- 25g flaked almonds
- 1 tsp cold pressed rapeseed oil
- 2 boneless, skinless chicken breasts (about 300g total)
- lime wedges, for squeezing

For the sauce
- 2 tsp cold pressed rapeseed oil
- 1 onion, roughly chopped
- 2 garlic cloves, finely chopped
- thumb-sized piece ginger, peeled and finely chopped
- 2 tsp medium curry powder
- 1 star anise
- ¼ tsp ground turmeric
- 1 tbsp wholemeal flour

For the rice
- 100g long-grain brown rice
- 2 spring onions, finely sliced (include the green part)

For the salad
- 1 carrot, peeled into long strips with a veg peeler
- ⅓ cucumber, peeled into long strips with a veg peeler
- 1 small red chilli, deseeded and finely chopped
- ½ lime, juiced
- small handful mint and/or coriander leaves

1 Heat the oven to 220C/200C fan/gas 7 or if using an air-fryer, heat to 180C for 4 mins. Cook the brown rice in plenty of boiling water for 35 mins or until tender.

2 Crush the almonds using a pestle and mortar or blitz in a food processor until finely chopped, then sprinkle over a plate. Grease a baking tray with a little of the oil, brush the chicken with the remaining oil and season. Coat with the nuts and place on the tray. Press any remaining nuts from the plate onto each breast. Bake for 20 mins in the oven or 18–20 mins in the air-fryer until browned and cooked through. Rest for 4–5 mins on the tray, then slice thickly.

3 Meanwhile, make the sauce. Heat the oil in a non-stick saucepan and add the onion, garlic and ginger. Loosely cover the pan and fry gently for 8 mins or until softened and lightly browned, stirring occasionally. Remove the lid for the final 2 mins, and don't let the garlic burn.

4 Stir in the curry powder, star anise, turmeric and a good grinding of black pepper. Cook for a few secondss more, stirring. Sprinkle over the flour and stir well. Gradually add 400ml water to the pan, stirring constantly.

5 Bring the sauce to a simmer and cook for 10 mins, stirring occasionally. If it begins to splutter, cover loosely with a lid. Remove from the heat and blitz the sauce with a stick blender until smooth. Adjust seasoning to taste. Keep warm.

6 Once the rice is tender, add the spring onions and cook for 1 min more. Drain well, then leave to stand for a few minutes while you make the salad. Toss the carrot and cucumber with the chilli, lime juice and herbs.

7 Divide the chicken between 2 plates, pour over the sauce and serve with the rice, salad and lime wedges.

Nutrition per serving:
Kcals 585, fat 16g, saturates 2g, carbs 58g, sugars 12g, fibre 9g, protein 47g, salt 0.3g

Tuna, caper & chilli spaghetti

Throw together tuna, capers and rocket with garlic, chilli and spaghetti to make this easy and healthy supper. It takes just 25 minutes to make.

 PREP 10 mins   COOK 15 mins   2

- 150g spaghetti or linguine
- 1 tbsp olive oil
- 1 garlic clove, sliced
- 1 red chilli, deseeded and finely chopped, plus extra to serve (optional)
- 1 tbsp drained capers
- small bunch parsley, finely chopped (stalks included)
- 145g tuna in spring water, drained
- 90g rocket or baby spinach leaves
- ½ lemon, juiced

1 Cook the spaghetti for 9–11 mins in a large pan of well-salted water until al dente.

2 Heat the oil in a wide frying pan over a very low heat, and gently cook the garlic and chilli to infuse the oil. Remove from the heat if the garlic is turning past light golden, as this will make it bitter.

3 Drain the pasta, keeping a cupful of the cooking water, and tip the spaghetti into the frying pan. Toss the pasta in the oil over a low heat, adding a little of the pasta water to emulsify into a sauce that coats the pasta, then fold in the capers, parsley, tuna and some seasoning. Don't stir too vigorously – you want to keep larger chunks of tuna. Toss the rocket and lemon juice through the spaghetti, and serve with extra chilli scattered over, if you like.

Nutrition per serving:
Kcals 409, fat 9g, saturates 1g, carbs 57g, sugars 2g, fibre 5g, protein 23g, salt 0.4g

Salmon & purple sprouting broccoli grain bowl

This bowl is full of omega-3, fibre and vitamin C. Check the mustard for ingredients. If there's anything that you wouldn't find in your kitchen, then it's likely a UPF – try the organic jars.

PREP 10 mins   COOK 10 mins   2

- 2½ tbsp cold pressed rapeseed oil
- ½ tsp honey
- ½ tsp wholegrain mustard
- 1 lemon, juiced
- 200g purple sprouting broccoli, each stem cut into 3 pieces
- 1–2 garlic cloves, sliced
- 250g pouch mixed grains
- handful parsley, roughly chopped
- handful dill, roughly chopped
- 160g radishes, cut into chunks
- 200g cooked salmon, broken into chunks

1 Mix 2 tbsp oil with the honey, mustard, lemon juice and some seasoning. Bring a pan of water to the boil. Add the broccoli, cook for 3–4 mins until tender but with a slight bite, then drain.

2 Heat the remaining oil in a frying pan. Add the garlic, sizzle for a minute, then tip in the mixed grain pouch, using the back of your spoon to separate the grains. Add the broccoli, mustard dressing, herbs and radishes. Give everything a mix to combine, season to taste, then gently stir through the salmon. Serve warm or cold.

Nutrition per serving:
Kcals 669, fat 39g, saturates 5g, carbs 36g, sugars 6g, fibre 10g, protein 39g, salt 0.4g

Simple mushroom curry

Serve these garlicky mushrooms in a rich tomato masala spiced with ground ginger, fennel seeds and cumin for an easy veggie supper. Enjoy with rice or homemade naan.

PREP 15 mins   COOK 40 mins   4

- 50g unsalted butter
- 500g chestnut mushrooms, quartered
- 4–6 tbsp cold pressed sunflower oil
- 1 tsp cumin seeds
- 1 tsp fennel seeds
- 1 large onion, finely chopped
- 4 garlic cloves, finely chopped
- 1 tsp ground ginger
- ¼ tsp ground turmeric
- ½ tsp Kashmiri chilli powder
- ½ tsp garam masala
- 400g can chopped tomatoes
- 1 tsp caster sugar
- 2 tbsp thick, full-fat Greek yogurt
- 2 tbsp chopped coriander
- cooked rice or homemade naan, to serve

1 Melt the butter in a large wok, karahi or non-stick frying pan over a medium–high heat and cook the mushrooms for 10 mins, or until any moisture has evaporated and they're starting to brown. Transfer to a bowl and set aside.

2 Heat the oil in the same pan over a medium–high heat and fry the cumin and fennel seeds, stirring continuously for about 30 seconds until they release a nutty aroma. Stir in the onion and cook for 12–15 mins until golden. Reduce the heat to medium, then add the garlic and continue frying for 1 min. Add the ginger, turmeric, chilli powder and garam masala, followed by the tomatoes and sugar. Cook, uncovered, for 5–7 mins, or until the masala thickens and a layer of oil forms around the edge of the pan.

3 Spoon the yogurt into a small bowl, add a small ladleful of the hot masala and mix well before stirring the yogurt into the pan of masala. Pour in 100ml hot water and simmer for 3–4 mins until the curry has the consistency of double cream. Season to taste, then return the mushrooms to the pan and stir to warm through. Scatter with the chopped coriander and serve with boiled rice or naan, if you like.

Nutrition per serving:
Kcals 302, fat 24g, saturates 10g, carbs 12g, sugars 10g, fibre 4g, protein 7g, salt 0.12g

Tomato penne with avocado

Get all 5 of your 5-a-day in this mildly spiced, healthy pasta dish. It's rich in iron, fibre and vitamin C as well as being low-fat and low-calorie.

PREP 10 mins   COOK 20 mins   2

- 100g wholemeal penne
- 1 tsp cold pressed rapeseed oil
- 1 large onion, sliced, plus 1 tbsp finely chopped
- 1 orange pepper, deseeded and cut into chunks
- 2 garlic cloves, grated
- 2 tsp mild chilli powder
- 1 tsp ground coriander
- ½ tsp cumin seeds
- 400g can chopped tomatoes
- 196g can sweetcorn in water
- 1 avocado, stoned and chopped
- ½ lime, zested and juiced
- handful coriander, chopped, plus extra to serve

1 Cook the pasta in salted water for 10–12 mins until al dente. Meanwhile, heat the oil in a medium pan. Add the sliced onion and pepper and fry, stirring frequently, for 10 mins until golden. Stir in the garlic and spices, then tip in the tomatoes, half a can of water and the corn and season well. Cover and simmer for 15 mins.

2 Meanwhile, toss the avocado with the lime juice and zest and the finely chopped onion.

3 Drain the penne and toss into the sauce with the coriander. Spoon the pasta into bowls, top with the avocado and scatter over the coriander leaves.

Nutrition per serving:
Kcals 485, fat 15g, saturates 3g, carbs 62g, sugars 26g, fibre 18g, protein 15g, salt 0.29g

Healthy chicken stir-fry

Make this nutritious stir-fry when you need dinner fast. When buying peanut butter, check the label to ensure it contains just peanuts and salt. And if you like a hit of spice, add chilli.

 PREP 10 mins   COOK 20 mins   2

- 65g brown basmati rice
- 2 tsp cold pressed rapeseed oil
- 15g ginger, peeled and cut into thin matchsticks
- 2 small red onions, cut into wedges
- 160g broccoli, broken into florets, stem finely chopped
- 2 carrots, halved lengthways, then cut into diagonal slices
- 1 red chilli, finely chopped (optional)
- 200g chicken breast, cut into thin strips
- ½ tsp ground cumin
- 1 tbsp crunchy peanut butter
- 1 tbsp wheat-free tamari
- 1 tbsp brown rice vinegar

1 Cook the rice following the pack instructions, then drain. Heat the oil in a non-stick wok over a high heat and fry the ginger and red onions for 2 mins. Add the broccoli stem, carrots and chilli, if using, and cook for 1 min.

2 Tip in the chicken and cumin, stir-fry briefly, then add the broccoli florets and 3 tbsp water. Cover and leave to steam for 3–4 mins, or until the broccoli florets are just tender and the chicken is cooked through.

3 Meanwhile, mix the peanut butter with the tamari and vinegar. Stir the sauce into the veg and chicken, then serve over the cooked rice.

Nutrition per serving:
Kcals 465, fat 13g, saturates 1g, carbs 47g, sugars 15g, fibre 10g, protein 35g, salt 1.3g

Creamy salmon, leek & potato traybake

Nestle leeks, potato and capers around salmon fillets to make this easy traybake for two. It's great as a midweek meal or for a more romantic occasion.

 PREP 5 mins   COOK 35 mins   2

- 250g baby potatoes, thickly sliced
- 2 tbsp olive oil
- 1 leek, halved, washed and sliced
- 1 garlic clove, crushed
- 70ml double cream
- 1 tbsp capers, plus extra to serve
- 1 tbsp chopped chives plus extra to serve
- 2 skinless salmon fillets
- mixed rocket salad, to serve (optional)

1 Heat the oven to 200C/180C fan/gas 6. Bring a medium pan of water to the boil. Add the potatoes and cook for 8 mins. Drain and leave to steam dry in a colander for a few minutes. Toss the potatoes with half the oil and plenty of seasoning in a baking tray. Put in the oven for 20 mins, tossing halfway through the cooking time.

2 Meanwhile, heat the remaining oil in a frying pan over a medium heat. Add the leek and fry for 5 mins, or until beginning to soften. Stir through the garlic for 1 min, then add the cream, capers and 75ml hot water and bring to the boil. Stir through the chives.

3 Heat the grill to high. Pour the creamy leek mixture over the potatoes, then sit the salmon fillets on top. Grill for 7–8 mins, or until just cooked through. Serve topped with extra chives and capers and a salad on the side, if you like.

Nutrition per serving:
Kcals 714, fat 52g, saturates 17g, carbs 20g, sugars 4g, fibre 5g, protein 39g, salt 0.5g

Chickpea stew with tomatoes & spinach

For a great night in, whip up this warming meal, serve with the homemade naan on page 20 and get comfy on the sofa.

PREP 10 mins   COOK 25 mins   4

- 1 tbsp cold pressed rapeseed oil
- 1 red onion, sliced
- 2 garlic cloves, chopped
- ½ finger-length piece ginger, shredded
- 2 mild red chillies, thinly sliced
- ½ tsp ground turmeric
- ¾ tsp garam masala
- 1 tsp ground cumin
- 4 tomatoes, chopped
- 2 tsp tomato purée
- 400g can chickpeas, rinsed and drained
- 200g baby spinach leaves
- rice or homemade naan bread, to serve

1 Heat the oil in a pan and fry the onion over a low heat until softened. Stir in the garlic, ginger and chillies and cook for a further 5 mins until the onions are golden and the garlic slightly toasted.

2 Add the turmeric, garam masala and cumin, stirring over a low heat for a few seconds. Tip in the tomatoes and add the tomato purée, then simmer for 5 mins.

3 Add the chickpeas to the pan with 300ml water (fill the can three-quarters full). Simmer for 10 mins before stirring in the spinach to wilt. Season and serve with rice or some homemade naan.

Nutrition per serving:
Kcals 145, fat 6g, saturates 0g, carbs 17g, sugars 6g, fibre 5g, protein 7g, salt 0.56g

Steaks with goulash sauce & sweet potato fries

Enjoy fillet steak with sauce for a healthy dinner that also boasts sweet potato fries, spinach and cherry tomatoes. You'll be getting all of your 5-a-day in this one.

 PREP 10 mins   COOK 25 mins   2

- 250g sweet potatoes, peeled and cut into narrow chips
- 1 tbsp thyme leaves
- 3 tsp cold pressed rapeseed oil, plus extra for the steaks
- 2 small onions, halved and sliced
- 1 green pepper, deseeded and diced
- 2 garlic cloves, sliced
- 1 tsp smoked paprika
- 85g cherry tomatoes, halved
- 1 tbsp tomato purée
- 2 x 125g fillet steaks, rubbed with a little rapeseed oil
- 200g baby spinach, wilted in a pan or the microwave

1 Heat the oven to 240C/220C fan/gas 7 and put a wire rack on top of a baking tray. Toss the sweet potatoes and thyme with 2 tsp oil in a bowl, then scatter them over the rack and set aside until ready to cook.

2 Heat 1 tsp oil in a non-stick pan, add the onions, cover the pan and leave to cook for 5 mins. Take off the lid and stir – they should be a little charred now. Stir in the green pepper and garlic, cover the pan and cook for 5 mins more. Put the potatoes in the oven and bake for 15 mins.

3 While the potatoes are cooking, stir the paprika into the onions and peppers, pour in 150ml water and stir in the cherry tomatoes and tomato purée and season well. Cover and simmer for 10 mins.

4 Pan-fry the steak in a hot, non-stick pan for 2–3 mins each side depending on their thickness. Rest for 5 mins. Spoon the goulash sauce onto plates and top with the beef. Serve the chips and spinach alongside.

Nutrition per serving:
Kcals 442, fat 14g, saturates 4g, carbs 42g, sugars 26g, fibre 12g, protein 33g, salt 0.4g

Charred broccoli, lemon & walnut pasta

Make this quick broccoli, lemon and walnut pasta with simple store cupboard ingredients. It's healthy, low in fat and calories and full of texture and flavour.

PREP 5 mins   COOK 15 mins   2

- 1 head broccoli, cut into small florets and stalk cut into small pieces
- 3 tsp olive oil
- 150g penne or fusilli
- 2 garlic cloves, crushed
- 1 tbsp roughly chopped walnuts
- pinch of chilli flakes
- ½ lemon, zested and juiced

1 Heat the grill to high. Put the broccoli on a baking tray and drizzle over 1 tsp of the oil. Season, and toss together. Grill for 8–10 mins, tossing around halfway through, until crispy and charred.

2 Cook the pasta in salted water following the pack instructions. Drain, reserving a cup of the cooking water.

3 In a frying pan, heat the remaining 2 tsp oil over a medium heat and fry the garlic, walnuts and chilli for 3–4 mins until golden.

4 Tip in the pasta, broccoli, lemon zest and juice, reserving a little of the zest. Add a splash of the reserved cooking water and toss everything together to coat the pasta. Serve in warmed bowls with the remaining lemon zest scattered over.

Nutrition per serving:
Kcals 435, fat 12g, saturates 2g, carbs 59g, sugars 4g, fibre 12g, protein 18g, salt 0.1g

Greek lamb meatballs

Prep these comforting Greek lamb meatballs with chargrilled veg and potatoes in just 5 minutes. A guaranteed family favourite, perfect for busy weeknights.

PREP 5 mins   COOK 35 mins   4

- 2 tbsp olive oil
- 500g lamb meatballs
- 300g baby new potatoes, thickly sliced
- 2 large garlic cloves, crushed
- 185g chargrilled vegetables, drained if in oil
- 2 x 400g cans chopped tomatoes with herbs
- 2 tsp light brown soft sugar
- 100g black olives
- 40g feta, crumbled
- ½ small bunch mint, finely shredded
- 1 lemon, zested

1 Heat 1 tbsp of the oil in a large shallow flameproof casserole or frying pan over a medium heat. Add the meatballs and fry for 5 mins or until golden brown. Set aside on a plate.

2 Heat the remaining oil in the same pan and fry the potatoes over a medium heat for 5 mins, or until they're starting to turn golden brown.

3 Add the garlic to the pan and fry for 1 min. Stir through the chargrilled veg, tomatoes and sugar, as well as the olives. Season. Add the meatballs back to the pan, cover and cook over a medium–low heat for 30–35 mins, stirring occasionally. Remove the lid halfway through – the potatoes should be just cooked through with the liquid slightly reduced.

4 Remove the pan from the heat and serve at the table with the feta, mint and lemon zest scattered over.

Nutrition per serving:
Kcals 555, fat 31g, saturates 11g, carbs 35g, sugars 12g, fibre 6g, protein 31g, salt 1g

Smoky cod, broccoli & orzo bake

Enjoy this one on busy weeknights. It's healthy, low in fat and since it's a traybake, there's minimal washing-up! If not using the stock recipe on page 8, check the packet ingredients.

PREP 10 mins   COOK 20 mins   2

- ½ tbsp olive oil, plus a drizzle
- 1 onion, chopped
- 1 tsp smoked paprika, plus a pinch
- ½–1 tbsp chipotle paste
- 200g long-stem broccoli
- 400ml fresh vegetable stock, hot
- 150g orzo
- ½ small bunch dill, chopped
- ½ small bunch parsley, chopped
- 50g frozen peas
- 2 skinless cod fillets
- 4 tbsp fat-free yogurt

1 Heat the oven to 200C/180C fan/gas 6. Heat the oil in a deep ovenproof frying pan and fry the onion for 5 mins until tender. Add the paprika, chipotle paste, broccoli and stock. Stir in the orzo, and transfer to the oven for 10 mins.

2 Stir in half the herbs and the peas, and nestle the fish into the orzo. Sprinkle over a pinch of paprika and drizzle with oil, then season. Cook for 8–10 mins until the fish is cooked and the orzo is tender. Mix the remaining herbs with the yogurt. Loosen with a little water if needed, then serve with the orzo and fish.

Nutrition per serving:
Kcals 618, fat 6g, saturates 1g, carbs 78g, sugars 18g, fibre 11g, protein 57g, salt 1.3g

Prawn fried rice

Make this easy Asian-inspired dish in just 30 minutes. It's healthy and low in calories but big on flavour, making it perfect for a speedy family supper.

🕐 PREP 5 mins   COOK 25 mins   🥧 4

- 250g long-grain brown rice
- 150g frozen peas
- 100g mangetout
- 1½ tbsp cold pressed rapeseed oil
- 1 onion, finely chopped
- 2 garlic cloves, crushed
- thumb-sized piece ginger, finely grated
- 150g raw king prawns
- 3 medium eggs, beaten
- 2 tsp sesame seeds
- 1 tbsp low-salt soy sauce
- ½ tbsp rice or white wine vinegar
- 4 spring onions, trimmed and sliced

1 Cook the rice following the pack instructions. Boil a separate pan of water and blanch the peas and mangetout for 1 min, then drain and set aside with the rice.

2 Meanwhile, heat the oil in a large non-stick frying pan or wok over a medium heat and fry the onion for 10 mins or until golden brown. Add the garlic and ginger and fry for a further minute. Tip in the blanched vegetables and fry for 5 mins, then the prawns and fry for a further 2 mins.

3 Stir the rice into the pan, then push everything to one side. Pour the beaten eggs into the empty side of the pan and stir to scramble them. Fold everything together with the sesame seeds, soy and vinegar, then finish with the spring onions scattered over.

Nutrition per serving:
Kcals 418, fat 11g, saturates 2g, carbs 54g, sugars 7g, fibre 6g, protein 22g, salt 0.5g

Sumac turkey-stuffed pittas

Pair subtly spiced meatballs with sweet-and-sour slaw for a vibrant dinner. This recipe takes just 25 minutes to make and is budget-friendly, too. Try making your own pittas (see page 14).

⏱ PREP 15 mins COOK 10 mins 🥧 2

- 300g turkey mince
- 1 tsp sumac
- 1 tsp ground cumin
- 1 garlic clove, crushed
- 1 lemon, zested and juiced
- 1 tbsp olive oil
- ¼ white cabbage, finely sliced
- small bunch mint, leaves picked and chopped
- ½ red onion, finely sliced
- ½ cucumber, deseeded and chopped
- 3 tbsp pomegranate seeds
- 2 large homemade pittas, toasted
- natural yogurt, to serve

1 Tip the mince, sumac, cumin, garlic and lemon zest into a bowl, season and combine using your hands. Form into 10 small balls, about 30g each. Heat the oil in a pan over a medium heat and fry the balls for 8–10 mins, shaking the pan now and then until browned and cooked.

2 Combine the cabbage, mint, onion, cucumber and pomegranate seeds with the lemon juice. Season. Stuff the slaw and meatballs into the pittas and serve with the yogurt.

Nutrition per serving:
Kcals 505, fat 16g, saturates 3g, carbs 43g, sugars 13g, fibre 8g, protein 44g, salt 0.8g

Chapter 6:
BATCH COOKING

Fill your freezer with recipes for batches that can be portioned up and frozen. Great to reach for instead of a ready meal on busy nights.

Pulled chicken & black bean chilli

Make a batch of this Mexican-inspired chicken chilli, which can easily be doubled and frozen. Check the label on the beans to make sure only beans and water are listed as the ingredients.

PREP 10 mins   COOK 1 hr   4

- 2 tbsp cold pressed sunflower oil
- 2 onions, sliced
- 4 boneless, skinless chicken thighs
- 3 garlic cloves, finely chopped
- pinch of sugar
- 1 tbsp oregano
- 1 tsp cumin seeds
- 3 tbsp chipotle in adobo or 1 tsp chipotle paste
- 350g passata
- 400g can black beans, drained but not rinsed
- ½ lime, juiced
- cooked rice or homemade tortillas, coriander, feta, lime wedges and chopped red onion, to serve (optional)

1 Heat the oil in a shallow saucepan or casserole dish with a lid. Tip in the onions and cook over a medium–low heat for 5 mins until softened. Add the chicken and turn up the heat to medium. Stir in the garlic, a small pinch of sugar, the oregano, cumin seeds and some seasoning. Cook for a couple of minutes, then add the chipotle and cook for a few minutes more. Pour in the passata and 100ml water. Season and bring to a simmer.

2 Cover with a lid and cook for 40–50 mins, stirring occasionally until the chicken is tender. Shred the chicken into the sauce using 2 forks, then stir through the beans. Simmer for 5 mins more, then turn off the heat. Squeeze in the lime juice. Can be kept chilled for 3 days and frozen for up to 2 months. Defrost thoroughly and reheat. Serve with rice or tortilla wraps and some coriander, feta, lime wedges and red onion on the side, if you like.

Nutrition per serving:
Kcals 254, fat 10g, saturates 2g, carbs 18g, sugars 8g, fibre 7g, protein 19g, salt 0.20g

One-pot prawn & lentil curry

Freeze the dhal base of this curry for busy weeknights, then simply defrost and add prawns, veg or meat. If not using the stock recipes on pages 8 or 9, check the packet ingredients.

PREP 30 mins   COOK 1 hr 50 mins   4

- 100g dried red lentils
- 3 tbsp cold pressed sunflower oil
- 1 large onion, finely chopped
- 6 garlic cloves, chopped or grated
- thumb-sized piece ginger, peeled and chopped or grated
- ¼ tsp ground turmeric
- ¼ tsp chilli powder (we used Kashmiri chilli powder)
- 1 tbsp cumin seeds
- 1 tbsp ground coriander
- 1 tbsp tomato purée
- 1 tsp lemon juice (optional)
- 400g can chopped tomatoes or passata
- 600ml fresh chicken or vegetable stock
- 1 tbsp garam masala
- 200g raw or cooked prawns (we used tiger prawns)
- green chillies, coriander and pickled red onions, to serve

1 Rinse the lentils a few times, then tip into a bowl, cover with cold water and leave to soak. Meanwhile, heat 2 tbsp oil in a shallow casserole or sauté pan, and cook the onion with a pinch of salt for 10 mins until it starts to turn golden. Add the garlic, ginger, turmeric, chilli powder, cumin seeds and ground coriander and cook for 3 mins until the mixture is sticky. Stir in the tomato purée and lemon juice, if using, followed by the chopped tomatoes. Simmer for 8–10 mins until you have a thick paste.

2 Rinse the soaked lentils again until the water runs clear, then drain. Stir the lentils into the tomato base, then tip in the stock (use some to swill out the tomato can). Bring to the boil, then reduce the heat to a gentle simmer, cover and cook, stirring occasionally, for 50 mins–1 hr, topping up with more water if needed, until the lentils are soft and have started to cook down into the sauce. Stir through the garam masala. This can now be left to cool completely, then chilled for up to 3 days or frozen for up to 6 months.

3 To cook the prawns, heat the sauce (defrost first if frozen) in a saucepan until simmering and cook for 10 mins, then tip in the prawns and cook for 5 mins. Season with salt to taste, then drizzle with the rest of the oil and stir briefly. Slice the green chillies and sprinkle these over with a few coriander leaves, then scatter with pickled onions to serve.

Nutrition per serving:
Kcals 282, fat 11g, saturates 1g, carbs 25g, sugars 9g, fibre 7g, protein 18g, salt 1.35g

Healthy beef ragu with baked potatoes

Use carrots, peas and passata to stretch a pack of mince in this healthier sauce, which provides 3 of your 5-a-day, Enjoy the ragu with jacket potatoes or pasta.

PREP 10 mins   COOK 40 mins   4

- 1 tbsp cold pressed rapeseed oil
- 2 large onions, halved or quartered, then sliced
- 3 large garlic cloves, finely grated
- 500g 5% fat steak mince
- 500g carton passata
- 3 carrots, finely chopped
- 1 tbsp thyme leaves
- ½ tsp ground white pepper
- 200g frozen peas
- 4 jacket potatoes, to serve

1 Heat the oil in a large non-stick pan over a medium–low heat and fry the onions for 10 mins, stirring occasionally until golden. Stir in the garlic, then add the mince and cook, breaking it up with a wooden spoon as you do, for a few minutes more until browned.

2 Add the passata, carrots, thyme and pepper, then season with salt. Cover and cook over a low heat for 25–30 mins, stirring occasionally until the meat is cooked and veg is tender. Add a splash of water to loosen, if you like, then stir in the peas and cook for 5–7 mins more until tender, seasoning to taste. Serve hot over jacket potatoes. Once completely cool, the mince sauce will keep frozen for up to 3 months. Defrost in the fridge overnight and reheat until piping hot.

Nutrition per serving:
Kcals 464, fat 9g, saturates 2g, carbs 56g, sugars 20g, fibre 13g, protein 35g, salt 0.27g

Moussaka

Make our easy moussaka for an instant crowd pleaser. This classic Greek dish of layered thinly sliced potato, aubergine and lamb is topped with a creamy béchamel sauce.

 PREP 30 mins   COOK 2 hrs 15 mins   8

- 6 tbsp olive oil
- 3 medium aubergines, cut into 5mm rounds
- 800g lamb mince
- 1 onion, finely chopped
- 2 fat garlic cloves, crushed
- 3 heaped tsp dried oregano
- 2 tsp ground cinnamon
- 2 bay leaves
- 200ml red wine
- 400g can chopped tomatoes
- 2 tbsp tomato purée
- ½ tbsp light brown soft sugar
- 550g Maris Piper potatoes, peeled and sliced into 5mm rounds

For the béchamel sauce
- 40g unsalted butter
- 40g plain flour
- 450ml whole milk
- 40g parmesan, finely grated
- grating of nutmeg
- 1 large egg plus 1 yolk, lightly beaten

1 Heat a frying pan over a high heat. Drizzle 4 tbsp of the oil over the aubergine and fry in batches for 5–7 mins or until golden and beginning to soften, adding more oil If they look a little dry. Set aside on a kitchen-paper-lined plate.

2 Heat 1 tbsp of the oil in a large flameproof casserole dish or pan over a medium–high heat. Add the mince and fry for 8–10 mins until a deep golden brown, regularly stirring and breaking up with a wooden spoon. Tip into a bowl. Add the remaining oil to the casserole, tip in the onion and a pinch of salt and fry gently for 10–12 mins until softened and turning translucent. Add the garlic, oregano, cinnamon and bay leaves and cook for 1 min. Return the lamb to the pan, pour in the red wine, bring to a bubble and reduce the wine by half. Stir through the tomatoes, tomato purée and brown sugar along with 200ml water. Season. Lower the heat and simmer gently, uncovered, for 20 mins, stirring occasionally until the sauce has thickened.

3 Heat the oven to 200C/180C fan/gas 4. Cook the potatoes in a large pan of lightly salted water for 6 mins, drain in a colander and leave to steam dry for 10 mins.

4 Melt the butter in a saucepan, stir in the flour and cook over a medium heat for 1 min. Remove from the heat and pour in the milk slowly, whisking until smooth. Return to the heat and simmer for 3 mins. Remove from the heat and whisk in the parmesan, nutmeg, seasoning and beaten egg.

5 Take a large rectangular ovenproof dish. Spoon in a third of the meat and spread out, followed by half the aubergine and potato, then the rest of the meat, a layer of aubergine followed by potato. Finish with the béchamel, smoothing the top. Cover and freeze at this point. Bake the moussaka (defrosted overnight if frozen) in the centre of the oven for 50 mins until deep golden brown. If it browns too much during cooking, cover the dish. Cool for 10 mins, then serve.

Nutrition per serving:
Kcals 516, fat 31g, saturates 13g, carbs 24g, sugars 9g, fibre 5g, protein 28g, salt 0.37g

Slow-cooked pork, cider & sage hotpot

A glorious hotpot ideal for storing in the freezer. Check the labels for the cider and stock (if you're not using the recipe on page 9) to ensure no unfamiliar extras have been added.

PREP 40 mins   COOK 3 hrs   6

- 4 tbsp olive oil, plus a little extra
- 1kg diced pork shoulder
- 20g butter, cubed, plus a little extra
- 4 leeks, trimmed and thickly sliced
- 4 garlic cloves, crushed
- 3 tbsp plain flour
- 500ml dry cider
- 400ml fresh chicken stock
- 2 bay leaves
- ½ small bunch parsley, finely chopped
- small bunch sage, leaves picked, 5 left whole, the rest chopped
- 200ml single cream
- 400g Maris Piper or King Edward potatoes
- 400g sweet potatoes

1 Heat half of the oil in a deep ovenproof frying pan or flameproof casserole dish, and fry the pork pieces over a medium–high heat in batches until seared all over, then transfer to a plate. Add another 1 tbsp oil to the pan, if you need to, while you're cooking the batches. Once all the pork is seared, transfer to a plate and set aside.

2 Add another 1 tbsp oil to the pan with a little butter and fry half the leeks with a pinch of salt for 10 mins until tender. Add the garlic, fry for a minute, then stir in the flour.

3 Pour in the cider, a little at a time, stirring to pick up any bits stuck to the bottom of the pan and to combine everything. Add the stock, bay leaves and seared pork, then simmer, half-covered with a lid for 1–1½ hrs until the meat is just tender (it will later cook to the point of falling apart in the oven). Can be prepared a day ahead.

4 Heat the oven to 200C/180C fan/gas 6. Simmer uncovered for a few minutes to reduce the sauce, if you need to – it shouldn't be too liquid or the potatoes will sink into the sauce. Stir in the parsley, chopped sage, remaining leeks, and the cream, then season well.

5 Peel both types of potatoes and cut into slices 2mm thick, by hand or using a mandoline. Alternate layers of potato and sweet potato in circles over the pie or randomly, if you prefer. Cover and freeze at this point. Dot the cubed butter over the top of the hotpot (defrosted overnight if frozen) and bake for 1–1½ hrs until the potato is tender. Nestle in the whole sage leaves, brushed in a little oil, for the last 10 mins. Leave to rest for 10 mins before serving.

Nutrition per serving:
Kcals 644, fat 35g, saturates 14g, carbs 39g, sugars 13g, fibre 80g, protein 35g, salt 0.6g

Slow-cooker ratatouille

Make up a batch of this slow-cooked ratatouille and freeze for easy midweek meals when you're busy. Packed with nutrients, it also delivers 4 of your 5-a-day.

PREP 10 mins   COOK 6 hrs 20 mins   6

- 2 tbsp olive oil
- 1 red onion, sliced
- 2 garlic cloves, crushed
- 2 large aubergines, cut into 1.5cm pieces
- 3 courgettes, halved and cut into 2cm pieces
- 3 mixed peppers, cut into 2cm pieces
- 1 tbsp tomato purée
- 6 large ripe tomatoes, roughly chopped
- small bunch basil, roughly chopped, plus a few extra leaves to serve
- few thyme sprigs
- 400g can plum tomatoes
- 1 tbsp red wine vinegar
- 1 tsp light brown soft sugar
- homemade bread, to serve (optional)

1 Heat the oil in a large frying pan and fry the onion for 8 mins until translucent. Add the garlic and fry for 1 min. Turn the heat to medium–high, add the aubergines and fry for 5 mins until golden. Stir in the courgettes and peppers and fry for 5 mins more until slightly soft. Add the tomato purée, fresh tomatoes, herbs, canned tomatoes, vinegar, sugar and 1 tsp salt and bring to the boil.

2 Transfer to the slow cooker and cook on Low for 5–6 hours or until everything is soft and the sauce has thickened. Season, scatter over some extra basil, and serve with homemade bread, if you like.

Nutrition per serving:
Kcals 162, fat 5g, saturates 1g, carbs 17g, sugars 16g, fibre 11g, protein 6g, salt 0.8g

Five-bean chilli

Batch-cook this vegan 5-bean chilli, then freeze in portions for busy weeknights. Check the label on the beans to make sure there are only beans and water listed in the ingredients.

PREP 5 mins   COOK 30 mins   4

- 1½ tbsp cold pressed rapeseed oil
- 1 onion, sliced
- 2 peppers, sliced
- 2 garlic cloves, crushed
- 1 tbsp ground cumin
- 1 tbsp ground coriander
- 2 tsp hot smoked paprika
- 400g can chopped tomatoes
- 400g can mixed beans, drained
- 400g can black beans, drained
- pinch of sugar
- 250g brown rice
- ½ small bunch coriander, chopped
- soured cream or guacamole, to serve (optional)

1 Heat the oil in a casserole dish and fry the onion and peppers for 10 mins over a medium heat until the onion is golden brown. Add the garlic and spices, and fry for 1 min. Pour in the tomatoes, both cans of beans, 50ml water, then add the sugar and season. Simmer, stirring regularly, for 15–20 mins until thickened.

2 Meanwhile, cook the rice following the pack instructions. Serve the chilli on the rice and scatter over the coriander. Top with a spoonful of soured cream or guacamole, if you like.

Nutrition per serving:
Kcals 439, fat 8g, saturates 1g, carbs 69g, sugars 10g, fibre 14g, protein 16g, salt 0.04g

Slow-cooker lamb stew

For the best texture, use boned shoulder or neck fillet in this stew for 8. You can freeze in individual containers. If not using the stock recipe on page 9, check the packet ingredients.

PREP 15 mins   COOK 4 hrs   8

- 1.5kg diced lamb shoulder
- 50g plain flour
- 2 tbsp cold pressed rapeseed oil
- 2 onions, roughly chopped
- 6 large carrots, halved lengthways and thickly sliced
- 2 garlic cloves, finely chopped
- 2 tbsp tomato purée
- 1.2l fresh chicken stock
- 2 bay leaves
- large rosemary sprig or a pinch of dried rosemary

1 Put the lamb and flour in a bowl, season and toss to coat. Heat the oil in a large frying pan or casserole over a medium heat, then fry in batches for 5–8 mins until browned all over. Tip the meat into the slow cooker. Add the onions and carrots to the pan and cook for 5–8 mins until starting to colour, then stir in the garlic and cook for 1 min more. Scatter in any leftover flour and stir for 1 min. Stir in the tomato purée and cook for a few minutes more.

2 Pour the stock over the veg, stir and bring to the boil. Pour the mix over the lamb. Nestle in the bay and rosemary, season and cook on High for 3–4 hrs, Medium for 5–6 hrs or Low for 7 hrs, stirring occasionally until the lamb is tender. Once cool, it can be frozen for 3 months. Defrost in the fridge fully and reheat in a pan until piping hot.

TIP
Elevate this simple stew with baked dumplings or turn it into a hotpot by topping with finely sliced potato and baking for up to 45 mins until hot and the potato is tender and golden.

Nutrition per serving:
Kcals 554, fat 36g, saturates 15g, carbs 13g, sugars 7g, fibre 3g, protein 43g, salt 0.4g

Cheese & onion pasties

Rustle up these pasties as an alternative to shop-bought ones. If you won't eat all 12, they freeze well and can be cooked from frozen. Be sure to check the mustard ingredients label.

PREP 30 mins   COOK 35 mins   Makes 10–12 pasties

- 1 tbsp cold pressed rapeseed oil
- 2 onions, sliced
- thyme sprigs, leaves picked
- 150g mature cheddar (or a mixture of strong hard cheeses), grated
- 1 tbsp wholegrain mustard
- 4 spring onions, sliced

For the pastry
- 250g plain flour, plus extra for dusting
- 125g cold butter
- large pinch of cayenne pepper
- ½ tsp English mustard powder
- 1 large egg, beaten

1 First, make the pastry. Tip the flour into a bowl. Holding the block of butter in its wrapper, grate it directly into the flour (you may need to dip the end of the butter into the flour occasionally if it becomes sticky). Add the cayenne pepper, mustard powder and half the beaten egg and season with a pinch of salt. Bring everything together with your hands until the mixture starts to clump. Tip the pastry onto the work surface and knead very briefly into a smooth ball, adding up to 3 tbsp cold water if it's too dry. Squash into a disc. Wrap and chill while you make the filling.

2 Heat the oil in a frying pan and cook the onions and thyme leaves for 8–10 mins until the onions have softened and started to caramelise. Tip into a bowl and leave to cool. Once cool, mix in the cheese, mustard and spring onions.

3 Heat the oven to 200C/180C fan/gas 6 and line a baking tray with baking parchment. Roll the chilled pastry out on a lightly floured surface to the thickness of a £1 coin. Cut out as many 10–12cm circles as you can (you can use a cup or mug as a template), then re-roll any off-cuts and repeat. You should get about 10–12 circles in total.

4 Spoon a mound of the filling into the centre of each pastry circle, leaving the edges clear. Working with one circle at a time, brush a little of the remaining beaten egg around the edge, then bring 2 sides up to meet in the middle in a half-moon shape. Pinch the pastry together, crimping the edge to seal. Transfer to the baking tray and repeat with the remaining pastry circles and filling. Brush all the pasties with some beaten egg. Will keep frozen for 2 months.

5 Bake the pasties for 20–25 mins (or 40–45 mins from frozen) until the pastry is deep golden brown. Leave to cool for at least 10 mins before eating warm, or cool completely and pack into containers for a picnic. Will keep in an airtight container for up to 3 days.

Nutrition per pasty (12):
Kcals 235, fat 15g, saturates 8g, carbs 18g, sugars 2g, fibre 1g, protein 6g, salt 0.5g

Slow-cooker pork casserole

Chopped apples would make a great addition – add in the final hour. If not using the stock on page 9, be sure to check the stock ingredients, as well as the mustard ingredients label.

🕐 PREP 15 mins   COOK 6–8 hrs   🥧 4

- 1 tbsp cold pressed rapeseed oil
- 4 pork shoulder steaks (about 750g), cut into large chunks
- 1 onion, chopped
- 1 leek, chopped
- 1 carrot, chopped
- bundle woody herbs (bouquet garni) – we used 2 bay leaves, 3 sage leaves and 4 thyme sprigs, plus a few thyme leaves to serve
- 2 tsp Dijon mustard
- 1 tbsp cider vinegar
- 500ml fresh chicken stock
- 2 tsp cornflour
- 1 tbsp honey

1 Heat your slow cooker. Drizzle the oil in a wide frying pan over a high heat. Season the pork, then add to the hot pan. Avoid overcrowding the meat – you may want to do this in batches. Cook until deep brown all over, then transfer to the slow cooker. Add the onion and leeks to the frying pan and cook for a few mins, until they soften. Add a splash of water and scrape any tasty bits from the bottom, then tip everything into the slow cooker. Add the carrot, herbs, mustard and vinegar, season, then add the stock and, if needed, pour over enough water to just cover the ingredients. Stir, then set your slow cooker on Low for 6–8 hrs or High for 5–6 hrs.

2 In a saucepan, mix the cornflour and honey with 1–2 tsp of liquid from the slow cooker until you have a smooth paste. Add 100ml more liquid, bring to a simmer until thickened, then stir back into the casserole. Serve with mash or dumplings, scattered with thyme leaves. If freezing, store in individual heatproof containers.

Nutrition per serving:
Kcals 429, fat 21g, saturates 7g, carbs 13g, sugars 10g, fibre 3g, protein 43g, salt 0.62g

Chapter 7:
FAMILY FAVOURITES

From flavour-packed meatballs to a black bean stew with cheddar dumplings, you won't miss any kinds of convenience foods with these easy meals the whole family will love.

Crispy fried chicken

· ·

If you love Southern-fried chicken, you'll be amazed by this UPF-free makeover. Check the panko to ensure it's just flour, yeast and salt or make your own from stale homemade bread.

🕐 PREP 15 mins plus 1 hr or overnight marinating   COOK 20 mins   🥧 4

- 150ml buttermilk
- 2 plump garlic cloves, crushed
- 4 boneless, skinless chicken breasts (about 550g total)
- 50g panko or coarse dried breadcrumbs
- 2 tbsp self-raising flour
- ½ rounded tsp paprika
- ¼ rounded tsp English mustard powder
- ¼ rounded tsp dried thyme
- ¼ tsp hot chilli powder
- ½ tsp ground black pepper
- 3 tbsp cold pressed rapeseed oil

1 Pour the buttermilk into a wide shallow dish and stir in the garlic. Slice the chicken into chunky slices, about 9.5cm long x 3–4cm wide. Lay the chicken in the dish and turn it over in the buttermilk so it is well coated. Leave in the fridge for 1–2 hrs, or preferably overnight.

2 Meanwhile, heat a large, non-stick frying pan and tip in the panko crumbs and flour. Toast them in the pan for 2–3 mins, stirring regularly so they brown evenly and don't burn. Tip the crumb mix into a bowl and stir in the paprika, mustard, thyme, chilli powder, pepper and a pinch of fine sea salt. Set aside.

3 When ready to cook, heat the oven to 230C/210C fan/ gas 8. Line a baking tin with foil and sit a wire rack (preferably non-stick) on top. Transfer half the crumb mix to a medium-large plastic bag. Lift half the chicken from the buttermilk, leaving the marinade clinging to it. Transfer it to the bag of seasoned crumbs. Seal the end of the bag and give it a good shake so the chicken gets well covered (you could do all the crumbs and chicken together if you prefer, but it's easier to coat evenly in 2 batches).

4 Remove the chicken from the bag. Heat 1 tbsp of the oil in a large, non-stick frying pan, then add the chicken pieces and fry for 1½ mins without moving them. Turn the chicken over, pour in another ½ tbsp of the oil to cover the base of the pan and fry for 1 min more, so both sides are becoming golden. Using tongs, transfer to the wire rack. Repeat with the remaining seasoned crumbs, oil and chicken.

5 Bake all the chicken on the rack for 15 mins until cooked and crisp, then serve with a homemade salad.

· ·

Nutrition per serving:
Kcals 319, fat 10.5g, saturates 1.1g, carbs 18.6g, sugars 2.2g, fibre 0.8g, protein 37.1g, salt 0.7g

Chipotle sweet potato & black bean stew with cheddar dumplings

Enjoy this stew with moreish cheese dumplings as a budget-friendly midweek meal. Check the label on the beans to make sure there are only beans and water listed in the ingredients.

 PREP 10 mins   COOK 50 mins   4

- cold pressed rapeseed oil, for frying
- 1 large red onion, finely sliced
- 250g diced butternut squash and sweet potato
- 400g can chopped tomatoes
- 2 x 400g cans chilli black beans or chilli kidney beans
- 3 tbsp chipotle chilli paste
- 125g self-raising flour
- 60g unsalted butter, cubed
- 70g mature cheddar, grated
- 1 large green jalapeño, finely sliced (optional)

1 Heat a glug of oil in a large flameproof casserole over a medium heat. Add the onion and a pinch of salt and cook for 7 mins until softened. Tip in the squash and sweet potato and fry for a few minutes before adding the tomatoes, beans and 250ml water. Stir through the chipotle paste and season to taste. Pop a lid on the dish and gently simmer over a low–medium heat for 25 mins or until reduced and the sweet potato is soft.

2 Heat the oven to 200C/180C fan/gas 6. Mix the flour with ½ tsp salt. Add the butter and rub together with your fingers until the mixture resembles fine breadcrumbs. Stir in the grated cheddar, then quickly mix in 4 tbsp cold water. Roll the mixture into 8 balls. Put the dumplings on top of the stew and place, uncovered, in the oven for 15–20 mins, or until puffed up and light golden brown. Serve the stew with the sliced jalapeño scattered on top, if you like.

Nutrition per serving:
Kcals 547, fat 23g, saturates 12g, carbs 60g, sugars 12g, fibre 15g, protein 18g, salt 1.5g

Frying pan pizza with aubergine, ricotta & mint

This recipe ensures a crispy-bottomed pizza without ever turning on the oven. It's got 2 of your 5-a-day too and it's UPF-free to boot! Ricotta can have additives, so check the labels.

 PREP 25 mins plus rising   COOK 35 mins   2

For the dough
- 200g strong white bread flour, plus a little for dusting
- ½ tsp fast-action dried yeast
- ¼ tsp golden caster sugar
- a little oil, for greasing

For the toppings
- 4 tbsp olive oil, plus a little extra
- 1 garlic clove, thinly sliced
- 200g passata
- pinch of golden caster sugar (optional)
- 1 small aubergine, sliced into discs
- 100g ricotta
- small handful mint, roughly chopped
- extra virgin olive oil, for drizzling

1 Weigh the ingredients for the dough into a large bowl and add ½ tsp salt and 125ml warm water. Mix to form a soft dough, then tip onto your work surface and knead for 5 mins or until the dough feels stretchy. Clean and grease the bowl and return the dough. Cover with a clean tea towel and leave somewhere warm to rise for 1 hr, or until the dough has doubled in size.

2 Meanwhile, make the sauce. Heat 1 tbsp olive oil in a pan and add the garlic. Sizzle gently for 30 secs, making sure the garlic doesn't brown, then add the passata. Season well and bubble for 8–10 mins until you have a rich sauce – add a pinch of sugar if it tastes a little too tart. Set aside.

3 When the dough has risen, knock out the air and roll it into a pizza base the same size as a large frying pan. Oil the surface of the dough, cover, then leave on the work surface for 15 mins to puff up a little. Meanwhile, heat 2 tbsp oil in the frying pan and add the aubergines in a single layer (you may have to cook in batches). Season well and cook for 4–5 mins on each side until really tender and golden. Transfer to a dish and cover with foil to keep warm.

4 Heat the remaining 1 tbsp of oil in the pan and carefully lift the dough into it. You may have to reshape it a little to fit. Cook over a low–medium heat until the underside is golden brown and the edges of the dough are starting to look dry and set – this should take about 6 mins, but it's best to go by eye. Flip over, drizzle a little more oil around the edge of the pan so it trickles underneath the pizza base, and cook for another 5–6 mins until golden and cooked through. Reheat the sauce if you need to and spread it over the base. Top with the warm aubergines and dot with spoonfuls of ricotta. Scatter with mint and drizzle with a little extra virgin olive oil just before serving.

Nutrition per serving:
Kcals 721, fat 31g, saturates 7g, carbs 85g, sugars 10g, fibre 9g, protein 20g, salt 1.4g

Butternut squash & cherry tomato crumble

Serve crumble for dinner by omitting the sugar and replacing the fruit with a savoury squash filling. It's a warming dish that's ideal for autumnal suppers.

PREP 20 mins   COOK 1 hr   6

- 1 tbsp olive oil
- 1 onion, finely chopped
- 1 garlic clove, finely chopped or grated
- 1 small butternut squash, peeled, deseeded and cut into bite-sized pieces
- 400g can cherry tomatoes
- 150g mascarpone
- 100g spinach

For the crumble
- 200g plain flour
- 125g cold butter, cut into cubes
- 50g parmesan (or vegetarian alternative), grated
- 50g cheddar, grated
- 50g walnuts, chopped
- few thyme sprigs, leaves picked

1 Heat the oven to 200C/180C fan/gas 6. Heat the oil in a large frying pan over a medium–low heat and fry the onion until softened but not coloured, about 10–12 mins. Stir in the garlic and cook for 1 min more before tipping in the squash. Cook for 8–10 mins until the squash has started to soften, then stir in the tomatoes, mascarpone and spinach. Season well and cook for a few minutes more to warm everything through, then tip into a medium baking dish (ours was 22 x 22cm).

2 For the crumble, rub the flour and butter together or blitz in a food processor to a breadcrumb-like consistency. Stir in the cheeses, walnuts and thyme and season. Scatter the crumble over the squash filling, being careful not to pack it down. Bake for 30–40 mins until the squash is tender and the crumble is golden.

Nutrition per serving:
Kcals 580, fat 42g, saturates 23g, carbs 36g, sugars 8g, fibre 4g, protein 13g, salt 0.7g

Slow-cooker meatballs

Try these slow-cooker meatballs for a tasty family meal. Turkey mince makes lighter meatballs, which kids and grown-ups love. They also freeze well if you want to batch cook.

🕐 PREP 1 hr   COOK 5 hrs   ◔ 4–5

- 1 tbsp cold pressed rapeseed oil, plus extra for the pan
- 1 onion, finely chopped
- 2 carrots, finely diced
- 2 celery sticks, finely diced
- 2 garlic cloves, thinly sliced
- 500g passata
- 2 tbsp roughly chopped parsley

For the meatballs
- 400g lean turkey mince
- 4 tbsp porridge oats
- pinch of paprika
- 1 garlic clove, crushed

1 Heat the slow cooker if necessary. Heat the oil in a non-stick frying pan and add the onion, carrots, celery and garlic and fry gently for a minute. Pour in the passata, add the parsley and stir, then transfer the lot to the slow cooker.

2 To make the meatballs, tip the mince into a large bowl. Add the oats, paprika, garlic and plenty of black pepper, and mix everything together with your hands. Divide the mixture into 20 lumps about the size of a walnut and roll each piece into a meatball. Heat a non-stick pan with a little oil and gently cook the meatballs until they start to brown. Add them to the tomato base and cook on Low for 5 hours. Serve over rice or pasta if you like, or with a green salad.

Nutrition per serving:
Kcals 260, fat 5g, saturates 1g, carbs 21g, sugars 10g, fibre 5g, protein 29g, salt 0.21g

Easy fish stew

This healthy one-pot is packed with fish, prawns and veg and is great for 2 or double to feed more. If not using the stock recipe on page 9, check the ingredients on the packaging.

 PREP 10 mins   COOK 20-25 mins   2

- 1 tbsp olive oil
- 1 tsp fennel seeds
- 2 carrots, chopped
- 2 celery sticks, chopped
- 2 garlic cloves, finely chopped
- 2 leeks, thinly sliced
- 400g can chopped tomatoes
- 500ml fresh chicken stock, heated to a simmer
- 2 skinless pollock fillets (about 200g), thawed if frozen, and cut into chunks
- 85g raw shelled king prawns

1 Heat the oil in a large pan, add the fennel seeds, carrots, celery and garlic, and cook for 5 mins until starting to soften. Tip in the leeks, tomatoes and stock, season and bring to the boil, then cover and simmer for 15–20 mins until the vegetables are tender and the sauce has thickened and reduced slightly.

2 Add the fish, scatter over the prawns and cook for 2 mins more until lightly cooked. Ladle into bowls and serve with a spoon.

Nutrition per serving:
Kcals 323, fat 10g, saturates 2g, carbs 19g, sugars 17g, fibre 11g, protein 35g, salt 0.57g

Tomato & mascarpone risotto

Double this up for a family. Switch mascarpone for cream cheese for a cheaper alternative and check packet ingredients for the cheese and stock (if not using the recipe on page 8).

 PREP 10 mins   COOK 30 mins   2

- 2 tbsp olive oil
- 1 onion, very finely chopped
- 1 large garlic clove, crushed
- 175g risotto rice
- 400g can cherry tomatoes
- 600ml fresh vegetable stock, hot
- 30g parmesan (or vegetarian alternative), grated
- 30g mascarpone or cream cheese
- ½ small bunch basil, chopped

1 Heat the oil in a large, heavy-based saucepan. Add the onion along with a pinch of salt, and fry for 10 mins or until beginning to soften and turn translucent, then add the garlic and fry for 1 min. Stir in the rice and cook for 2 mins.

2 Tip in the tomatoes and bring to a simmer. Add half the stock, cooking and stirring until absorbed. Add the remaining stock, a ladleful at a time, and cook until the rice is al dente, stirring constantly for around 20 mins.

3 Stir through the parmesan, mascarpone or cream cheese and basil, then season to taste. Spoon into bowls to serve.

Nutrition per serving:
Kcals 635, fat 24g, saturates 9g, carbs 86g, sugars 14g, fibre 6g, protein 16g, salt 0.3g

One-pot garlic chicken

You can adjust the amount of garlic to suit your own tastes in this and a one-pot saves on washing-up! If not using the stock recipe on page 9, check the ingredients on the packaging.

PREP 10 mins   COOK 30 mins   4

- 4 medium boneless, skinless chicken breasts, sliced crossways into thick strips
- 75g plain flour
- 2 tbsp olive oil
- 50g unsalted butter
- 10–15 small garlic cloves, or to taste
- 250ml fresh chicken stock, hot
- 100ml double cream
- 30g parmesan, finely grated
- small bunch flat-leaf parsley, finely chopped (optional)
- cooked rice and steamed green beans, to serve

1 Tip the chicken into a shallow bowl and sprinkle over the flour. Season well. Heat the oil in a large frying pan over a medium–high heat and fry the chicken, shaking off any excess flour first, for 1–2 mins until lightly golden all over. (You may need to do this in batches.)

2 Reduce the heat to medium and add the butter. Peel as many garlic cloves as you prefer, and drop these into the pan. Cook for 5 mins until the garlic has turned lightly golden, stirring to keep the chicken from burning.

3 Pour in the stock and simmer for 10 mins until the garlic is tender. Add the cream and cheese and simmer for a further 5 mins until the sauce thickens slightly. Taste for seasoning and adjust as needed. Scatter with the chopped parsley, if using, and serve hot with rice and green beans, if you like.

Nutrition per serving:
Kcals 570, fat 36g, saturates 17g, carbs 17g, sugars 1g, fibre 1g, protein 44g, salt 0.69g

Easy lamb tagine

Sweet, juicy apricots and tender butternut squash are a winner with kids and adults alike. If not using the stock recipe on page 8, be sure to check the packet ingredients.

🕐 PREP 10 mins   COOK 2 hrs 10 mins   🥧 4–6

- 2 tbsp olive oil
- 1 onion, finely diced
- 2 carrots, finely diced
- 500g diced leg of lamb
- 2 fat garlic cloves, crushed
- ½ tsp ground cumin
- ½ tsp ground ginger
- ¼ tsp saffron strands
- 1 tsp ground cinnamon
- 1 tbsp clear honey
- 100g soft dried apricots, quartered
- 500ml fresh vegetable stock, hot
- 1 small butternut squash, peeled, seeds removed and cut into 1cm dice
- steamed couscous or rice, to serve
- chopped parsley and toasted pine nuts, to serve (optional)

1 Heat the oil in a heavy-based pan and add the onion and carrot. Cook for 3–4 mins until softened. Add the diced lamb and brown all over. Stir in the garlic and all the spices and cook for a few minutes more or until the aromas are released.

2 Add the honey and apricots, and pour over the stock. Give it a good stir and bring to the boil. Turn down to a simmer, put the lid on and cook for 1 hr.

3 Remove the lid and cook for a further 30 mins, then stir in the squash. Cook for 20–30 mins more until the squash is soft and the lamb is tender. Serve alongside rice or couscous and sprinkle with parsley and pine nuts, if using.

Nutrition per serving (4):
Kcals 413, fat 21.7g, saturates 7.5g, carbs 27.3g, sugars 22.4g, fibre 6.4g, protein 27.2g, salt 1g

Homemade beef burgers

Learn how to make succulent burgers with just 4 ingredients. An easy recipe for perfect homemade patties with beef mince. See the recipe on page 18 for homemade burger buns.

 PREP 15 mins plus chilling   COOK 15 mins   4

- 500g good-quality beef mince
- 1 small onion, diced
- 1 egg
- 1 tbsp cold pressed rapeseed oil
- 4 homemade burger buns, sliced in half

To serve
- sliced tomato, sliced red onion, sliced gherkins, handful shredded iceberg lettuce

1 Tip the mince into a bowl with the onion and egg and season well, then mix. Divide the mixture into 4. Lightly wet your hands. Carefully roll the mixture into balls, each about the size of a tennis ball. Set in the palm of your hand and gently squeeze down to flatten into patties about 3cm thick. Make sure all the burgers are the same thickness so that they will cook evenly. Put on a plate, cover and leave in the fridge to firm up for at least 30 mins.

2 Heat a griddle pan or frying pan over a medium–high heat. Lightly brush one side of each burger with the oil and put the burgers, oil-side down, on the pan. Cook for 5–7 mins, until the meat is well browned. Don't move them around or they may stick. Brush the oil over the other side, then turn over. Don't press down on the meat, as that will squeeze out the juices. Cook for 5–7 mins until cooked through. Remove to a plate and leave to rest.

3 Put the pan over a medium heat and add the buns, cut-side down, and toast for 1–2 mins until browned. Place a burger inside each bun, then top with your choice of accompaniment.

Nutrition per serving:
Kcals 562, fat 28g, saturates 10g, carbs 41g, sugars 3g, fibre 2g, protein 35g, salt 1.47g

Chapter 8:
WEEKEND FEASTS

Whether you're entertaining or just want to go all out on the weekend, you're sure to find to a dish to suit the occasion in this chapter.

Ratatouille tart with flaky cheddar & thyme pastry

Bake cheesy puff pastry topped with a smoky aubergine and tomato compote and roasted courgettes for this stunning tart. This is ideal for an al fresco lunch with friends.

PREP 40 mins plus overnight freezing and at least 30 mins chilling COOK 1 hr 30 mins   8–10

- 5 medium tomatoes (a mixture of different colours looks nice), sliced to a £1 thickness
- 1 aubergine
- 2 tbsp olive oil
- 2 red onions, sliced
- 4 garlic cloves, crushed
- 1 tbsp caster sugar
- 2 courgettes (we used 1 green and 1 yellow), sliced to a £1 thickness
- 20g parmesan (or vegetarian alternative), grated

For the pastry
- 300g plain flour, plus extra for dusting
- 4 tbsp polenta
- 50g extra mature cheddar, coarsely grated
- small bunch thyme, leaves picked (reserve a few for garnish)
- 150g butter (freeze in foil overnight to make it easier to grate)
- 1 egg yolk, beaten (freeze the white for another recipe)

1 For the pastry, mix the flour with half the polenta and the cheese, thyme and a pinch of salt. Grate in the butter, handling as little as possible and stirring it in with a knife as you go. Give it one last stir so all the butter is coated with flour, then quickly stir in 125ml very cold water. Gently bring together with your hands, splashing in a little more water if it looks dry, then wrap in baking parchment and chill for 30 mins.

2 Reserve half the tomato slices, then roughly chop the rest. Heat the grill to high. Pierce the aubergine 4–5 times and grill, turning often, for 8–10 mins until the skin is charred and the aubergine is soft. Leave to cool, then scrape off the skin (don't worry if a few bits stick) and roughly chop the flesh.

3 Heat half the oil in a pan over a low–medium heat and cook the onions with a pinch of salt for 10 mins until starting to caramelise. Add the garlic and aubergine and cook for another 5 mins until any liquid has evaporated. Add the chopped tomatoes and sugar, season, and cook for 5–10 mins until thickened. Leave to cool. Put the courgettes in a bowl and toss with a good pinch of salt. Leave for 10 mins.

4 Heat the oven to 200C/180C fan/gas 6 with a baking tray inside. Roll the pastry out on a large sheet of parchment dusted with a little flour to a circle about 35cm wide. Trim the edge. Drain the courgettes and pat dry with kitchen paper. Sprinkle the remaining polenta over the pastry, then spread over the cooled tomato mix, leaving a 3cm border. Arrange the tomato slices and courgettes in overlapping circles on top of the tart. Brush with the remaining oil, season and sprinkle with parmesan. Fold the pastry edge over the veg slightly, pressing gently to seal. Brush the edge with the beaten yolk. Carefully slide the tart, still on the parchment, onto the hot tray. Bake for 45 mins until golden, then scatter with thyme. Leave to cool a little and serve just warm or at room temperature.

Nutrition per serving (10):
Kcals 346, fat 18g, saturates 10g, carbs 35g, sugars 7g, fibre 4g, protein 8g, salt 0.4g

Chicken Provençal

Cater for a crowd with a casserole that evokes summer in Provence with its herbs, tomatoes, olives and artichokes. If not using the stock recipe on page 9, check the packet ingredients.

PREP 15 mins plus at least a few hrs marinating   COOK 1 hr 40 mins   5–6

- 2.5kg chicken, jointed (ask your butcher to do this)
- 8 garlic cloves, thinly sliced
- 200ml white wine
- 4 tbsp olive oil
- 1 tsp thyme leaves
- 10 ripe plum tomatoes, halved
- 1 tbsp tomato purée
- ½ tsp herbes de Provence
- 1 tbsp fennel seeds
- 500ml fresh chicken stock
- 1 celery stick, finely diced
- 15 button or silverskin onions, or small shallots, peeled
- 285g jar chargrilled artichoke hearts, drained
- 100g pitted green olives

1 Tip the chicken into a large bowl or dish and add the garlic, wine, 2 tbsp oil and the thyme. Season with 2 tbsp flaky salt and mix well until completely coated. Cover and chill for at least a few hours, but preferably overnight.

2 Heat the grill to high. Arrange the plum tomatoes on a tray, cut-side up, drizzle with 1 tbsp oil and grill for 15 mins, or until charred. Set aside.

3 Heat 1 tbsp oil in a large casserole dish or flameproof roasting tin. Scrape the marinade off the chicken pieces back into the bowl and fry the chicken in batches for about 15 mins until the skin is golden and crisp – watch out, the oil has a tendency to sputter. Remove the chicken from the dish and pour off the oil. Place the dish back on the heat, add the tomato purée and cook for 2 mins, then add the herbs, fennel seeds, remaining marinade and chicken stock. Bring up to the boil, add the grilled tomatoes, then simmer gently for 20 mins.

4 Heat the oven to 160C/140C fan/gas 4. Nestle the chicken pieces back into the dish, then stir them in to coat in the sauce. Scatter over the celery, button onions and artichokes. Bring up to a simmer, pop the lid on, then transfer to the oven and cook for 1 hr. Remove the lid and stir in the olives. Season to taste and leave everything to settle for 15 mins before serving straight from the dish.

Nutrition per serving (5):
Kcals 507, fat 30g, saturates 7g, carbs 10g, sugars 8g, fibre 5g, protein 39g, salt 2.3g

Baked camembert dough ball platter

The ultimate easy-going food for a crowd: a tear-and-share dough ball platter, served with rosemary-spiked gooey cheese, ready for some serious dipping.

PREP 1 hr plus proving   COOK 30 mins   12–15

- 115g unsalted butter, chopped
- 600g strong white bread flour
- 7g fast-action dried yeast, plus another ½ tsp
- 2 tsp golden caster sugar
- drizzle of olive oil, for greasing
- 2 tbsp fine polenta or cornmeal
- 3 x 250g boxes camembert
- small handful woody herbs, such as rosemary and thyme (optional)
- 1 egg, beaten
- 3 tbsp poppy seeds
- 3 tbsp sesame seeds

1 Warm 350ml water in a saucepan until steaming, then remove from the heat, add the butter and set aside to cool until you can comfortably put your finger in the liquid. Combine the flour, yeast, sugar and 1 tsp salt in a large bowl or the bowl of a stand mixer. Add the cooled liquid and combine to make a soft dough. Knead for 10 mins by hand, or 5 mins in a mixer, until the dough feels stretchy and smooth. Return to a clean, oiled bowl and cover. Leave somewhere warm to rise for 1½–2 hrs or until doubled in size.

2 Grease and line your largest baking tray (ours was 42 x 33cm) with baking parchment. Grease the parchment too, then scatter over the polenta. Remove the cheeses from their boxes and place on the tray, spaced well apart. Brush each one with a little oil, slash the tops a few times with a sharp knife and poke in some fresh herbs, if you like.

3 Pour the egg into a shallow dish, the poppy seeds in another and the sesame in a third. Knock the air out of the dough and knead again for several minutes. Take a small piece of dough (about the size of a whole walnut) and roll it into a ball. Dip the top in egg, then into one of the dishes of seeds, and place on the baking tray, seeded-side up. Continue rolling and dunking the dough, leaving every third piece seedless, filling the tray but leaving a little space between each ball of dough. When you have used all the dough, you may need to reposition the dough balls to ensure the baking tray is evenly covered.

4 Heat the oven to 180C/160C fan/gas 4. Cover the tray with a clean tea towel and leave for 30 mins–1 hr until the dough has doubled in size and the balls are touching. Bake for 25–30 mins until the dough balls are cooked through and the cheese is oozy and melted. Leave to cool for 5 mins, then serve.

Nutrition per serving (15):
Kcals 377, fat 20g, saturates 12g, carbs 31g, sugars 1g, fibre 1g, protein 17g, salt 1.1g

Chicken cacciatore one-pot with orzo

The orzo soaks up the flavours of the chicken and tomatoes as it cooks, making a wonderfully rich pasta bake. If not using the stock recipe on page 9, check the packet ingredients.

PREP 5 mins plus resting   COOK 55 mins   4

- 2 tbsp olive oil
- 4–6 skin-on, bone-in chicken thighs
- 1 onion, finely sliced
- 2 garlic cloves, sliced
- 250ml red wine
- 2 bay leaves
- 4 thyme sprigs
- few rosemary sprigs
- small bunch parsley, stalks and leaves separated, finely chopped
- 2 x 400g cans cherry tomatoes
- 300ml fresh chicken stock
- 1 tbsp balsamic vinegar
- 2 tbsp capers (optional)
- handful pitted green olives
- 300g orzo, rinsed (to keep it from getting too sticky when baked)

1 Heat the oven to 220C/200C fan/gas 7. Rub 1 tbsp oil over the chicken and season well, then put skin-side up in an ovenproof casserole dish or roasting tin and bake for 20–25 mins until crisp and golden, but not cooked all the way though. Remove from the dish and put on a plate.

2 Add the remaining oil to the dish, mixing it with the chicken fat. Tip in the onion and garlic, then bake for 5–8 mins until the onion is tender.

3 Pour in the wine, stirring it with the onions, then leave to evaporate slightly in the residual heat before adding the bay, thyme, rosemary, parsley stalks and tomatoes. Pour in the chicken stock, then add the vinegar, capers, if using, olives and orzo. Stir well and season.

4 Nestle the chicken back in the pan, skin-side up, and roast for 20 mins until the sauce is thickened, the orzo is tender and the meat is cooked through. Give it a stir, then leave for 10 mins for the orzo to absorb the excess liquid. Scatter over the parsley leaves to serve.

Nutrition per serving:
Kcals 618, fat 19g, saturates 4g, carbs 68g, sugars 12g, fibre 6g, protein 29g, salt 1.1g

One-pot chicken & mushroom risotto

Risotto is the ultimate one-pot supper – the perfect vehicle for letting simple, comforting ingredients shine. If not using the stock recipe on page 9, check the packet ingredients.

 PREP 15 mins   COOK 35 mins   4

- 60g butter
- 1 large onion,
  finely chopped
- 2 thyme sprigs,
  leaves picked
- 250g chestnut mushrooms,
  sliced
- 300g risotto rice
- 1.5l fresh chicken stock, hot
- 200g cooked chicken,
  chopped into chunks
- 50g parmesan, grated, plus
  extra to serve (optional)
- small bunch parsley,
  finely chopped

1 Heat the butter in a large pan over a gentle heat and add the onion. Cook for 10 mins until softened, then stir in the thyme leaves and mushrooms. Cook for 5 mins, sprinkle in the rice and stir to coat in the mixture.

2 Ladle in a quarter of the stock and continue cooking, stirring occasionally and topping up with more stock as it absorbs (you may not need all the stock).

3 When most of the stock has been absorbed and the rice is nearly cooked, add the chicken and stir to warm through. Season well and stir in the parmesan and parsley. Serve scattered with extra parmesan, if you like.

Nutrition per serving:
Kcals 615, fat 21g, saturates 12g, carbs 67g, sugars 5g, fibre 5g, protein 37g, salt 1.5g

Beetroot hummus party platter

This one-platter-serves-all beetroot hummus will be a big hit if you have friends over and doesn't require cooking. Serve with homemade bread or rolls (see pages 16 and 18).

PREP 15 mins   6

- 2 x 400g cans chickpeas, drained
- 2 x 300g packs cooked beetroot, drained
- 2 small garlic cloves
- 2 tbsp tahini
- 100ml extra virgin olive oil, plus a drizzle to serve
- good squeeze of lemon juice
- 2 tbsp toasted hazelnuts, roughly chopped
- 2 tbsp pumpkin seeds, roughly chopped
- 2 tsp nigella seeds
- 1 tsp sumac (optional)
- pinch of chilli flakes (optional)

To serve (optional)
- crunchy summer veg, cut into batons (we used fennel, sugar snap peas, baby heritage carrots and radishes)
- homemade bread, toasted and cut into fingers for dipping
- mini mozzarella balls
- olives

1 Set about 2 tbsp chickpeas aside. Tip the rest of the chickpeas, the beetroot, garlic, tahini, oil and lemon juice into a food processor with a good pinch of salt. Blend until smooth, then check the seasoning, adding a little more salt or lemon if it needs it. Chill the hummus until you're ready to serve (it will keep for up to 2 days).

2 Transfer the hummus to a wide, shallow bowl or spread over a platter. Drizzle with some oil, scatter with the reserved chickpeas, hazelnuts, seeds, sumac and chilli (if using). Arrange the crunchy veg and other accompaniments around the platter and let everyone dig in.

Nutrition per serving (only for hummus, no nuts, seeds or optionals):
Kcals 312, fat 22g, saturates 3g, carbs 17g, sugars 7g, fibre 6g, protein 9g, salt 0.2g

Slow-roast lamb with prunes & roasted garlic

Tuck into slow-roasted lamb for Sunday lunch, with a delicious marinade made with prunes, pomegranate molasses and spices. Pair with boulangère potatoes to impress your guests.

PREP 20 mins plus at least 50 mins marinating and resting   COOK 4 hrs 45 mins   6-8

- 2 whole garlic bulbs
- 2 tbsp olive oil, plus extra for drizzling
- 1 whole lamb shoulder, approx 2.5kg
- 1½ tbsp plain flour or cornflour
- 150ml white wine

For the marinade
- 12 dried prunes
- 2 tbsp pomegranate molasses
- 1 tsp ground turmeric
- 1 tsp ground cumin
- 2 tsp ground black pepper
- ½ tbsp dried thyme
- 1 tsp salt

1 Heat the oven to 180C/160C fan/gas 4. Remove any loose skin from the garlic bulbs and slightly fan the cloves without removing them from the root. Put on a sheet of foil, then drizzle with the 2 tbsp oil and sprinkle with salt. Wrap in the foil, and roast in the oven for 30–35 mins until soft. Leave to cool.

2 For the marinade, put the prunes in a jug with 100ml boiling water for 10 mins until soft. Squeeze the roasted garlic flesh from the skins into the jug, then add the rest of the marinade ingredients. Whizz together using a hand blender until smooth.

3 Put the lamb in a large baking dish. Make small incisions with a sharp knife, then pour the marinade over, massaging it into the holes. Cover with foil and leave to marinate in the fridge for at least 30 mins or up to 24 hrs.

4 Turn the temperature up to 200C/180C fan/gas 6 and put the lamb in the oven, immediately turning it down to 150C/130C fan/gas 2. Cook for 3–4 hrs, until the lamb has pulled away from the bone. Remove from the oven.

5 Pour the juices into a jug, then skim off the layer of fat. Turn the grill to high, then brown the lamb for 10 mins. Remove, loosely cover with the foil, and rest for 20 mins before shredding the meat.

6 Add 1½ tbsp of the juices to a saucepan over a medium heat and mix in the flour or cornflour. Cook for 3 mins, stirring, until it starts to colour, then add the wine and simmer to reduce the liquid by half. Stir in the remaining meat juices. Taste for seasoning, then serve with the lamb.

Nutrition per serving (8):
Kcals 485, fat 25g, saturates 11g, carbs 13g, sugars 8g, fibre 2g, protein 47g, salt 1g

Baked sea bass with lemon caper dressing

This elegant, gluten-free main is special enough for a dinner party, yet simple and quick to make for no-fuss entertaining. Be sure to check the mustard ingredients label.

 PREP 10 mins COOK 10 mins   4

- 4 x 100g sea bass fillets
- olive oil, for brushing

For the caper dressing
- 3 tbsp extra virgin olive oil
- 1 lemon, zested, plus 2 tbsp juice
- 2 tbsp small capers
- 2 tsp Dijon mustard
- 2 tbsp chopped flat-leaf parsley, plus a few extra leaves (optional)

1 To make the dressing, mix the oil with the lemon zest and juice, capers, mustard, some seasoning and 1 tbsp water. Don't add the parsley yet (unless serving straight away) as the acid in the lemon will fade the colour if they are left together for too long.

2 Heat the oven to 220C/200C fan/gas 7. Line a baking tray with baking parchment and put the fish, skin-side up, on top. Brush the skin with oil and sprinkle with some flaky salt. Bake for 7 mins or until the flesh flakes when tested with a knife. Arrange the fish on warm serving plates, spoon over the dressing and scatter with extra parsley leaves, if you like.

Nutrition per serving:
Kcals 196, fat 13g, saturates 2g, carbs 1g, sugars 1g, fibre 0g, protein 20g, salt 0.8g

Hasselback butternut squash with tahini yogurt & gremolata

Enjoy our hasselback butternut squash as a showstopping veggie main. It's spiced with cinnamon and nutmeg, and served with a zingy citrus and herb gremolata.

PREP 20 mins   COOK 1 hr   6 as a main or 10–12 as a side

- 3 medium butternut squash, halved vertically, peeled and deseeded
- 6 star anise
- 5 tbsp olive oil
- 1 tsp ground cinnamon
- ½ nutmeg, grated
- 3 tbsp light brown soft sugar
- 100g natural yogurt
- 100g tahini
- 1 lemon, zested and juiced

For the gremolata
- 2 large handfuls flat-leaf parsley, leaves picked and finely chopped
- 1 orange, zested, plus ½ juiced
- 1 garlic clove, crushed
- 3 tbsp dried cranberries
- 4 tbsp pomegranate seeds
- 5 tbsp flaked almonds, toasted

1 Heat the oven to 200C/180C fan/gas 6. Working with one squash half at a time, put on a chopping board with a wooden spoon on either side. Using a large, sharp knife, cut slices crossways along the length of the squash at ½cm intervals, cutting through only until you reach the spoon handles. Arrange the squash on 2 baking trays lined with baking parchment, flat-side down. Drop a star anise into the cavity of each half, then drizzle over 3 tbsp of the olive oil. Combine the cinnamon, nutmeg and brown sugar, then rub this all over the squash halves. Roast for 45 mins until soft, basting with any roasting juices after 30 mins. If the squash starts to burn, cover loosely with foil and return to the oven. Leave to cool slightly.

2 Meanwhile, make the gremolata. Put the parsley in a small bowl and mix with the rest of the olive oil, the orange zest and juice, garlic, dried cranberries and pomegranate seeds. Set aside.

3 Mix the yogurt and tahini with the lemon zest and juice in a separate bowl. Season and stir in 1–4 tbsp water to loosen until it's the consistency of double cream.

4 Just before serving, stir the almonds through the gremolata. Arrange the roasted squash halves on a serving platter, then top with the tahini yogurt and gremolata.

Nutrition per serving (6):
Kcals 483, fat 27g, saturates 4g, carbs 45g, sugars 33g, fibre 9g, protein 11g, salt 0.1g

Chicken paprikash

A traditional Hungarian casserole that's perfect for relaxed entertaining. Enjoy with potatoes, noodles or rice. If not using the stock recipe on page 9, check the packet ingredients.

PREP 15 mins   COOK 50 mins–1 hr   4–6

- 8 skin-on, bone-in chicken thighs
- 1 tbsp cold pressed rapeseed oil
- 2 onions, finely chopped
- 2 red or green peppers (or a mixture), chopped
- 2 garlic cloves, crushed or finely grated
- 3 large ripe tomatoes (around 400g), deseeded and chopped, or 1 x 400g can chopped tomatoes
- 1½ tbsp plain flour
- 3 tbsp sweet smoked paprika
- 1 tbsp hot paprika (optional)
- 350ml fresh chicken stock
- 200ml soured cream
- boiled potatoes, noodles or rice, to serve

1 Season the chicken thighs. Heat the oil in a large saucepan over a medium heat and fry the thighs in batches for 5–8 mins until browned all over. Remove from the pan and set aside. Tip in the onion and fry for 8–10 mins until softened and turning golden.

2 Stir in the peppers and cook for 3 mins, then add the garlic and tomatoes. Cook for another 5–8 mins until the tomatoes have started to break down. Sprinkle in the flour, paprika and hot paprika, if using, and cook for 30 seconds more. Return the chicken thighs to the pan and mix gently to coat.

3 Pour in the stock, bring to the boil, then turn down the heat and simmer, covered, for 15 mins. Remove the lid and simmer for another 15 mins until the sauce has thickened. Stir in the soured cream and cook for 5 mins – the sauce should be quite thick. Serve with boiled potatoes, noodles or rice.

Nutrition per serving (6):
Kcals 468, fat 23g, saturates 8g, carbs 15g, sugars 11g, fibre 5g, protein 46g, salt 0.55g

Chapter 9:
PUDDINGS & BAKES

You won't be tempted by the cakes aisle in the supermarket after browsing these recipes! From autumnal pumpkin muffins to lemon drizzle sponge pudding, there's a treat in here for everyone.

Carrot cake cupcakes

This crowd-pleasing recipe turns an afternoon tea classic into dainty cupcakes. Be sure to check the vanilla extract and soft cheese ingredients to avoid UPFs.

PREP 30 mins   COOK 22 mins   Makes 12 cupcakes

- 175g light brown muscovado sugar
- 100g wholemeal self-raising flour
- 100g self-raising flour
- 1 tsp bicarbonate of soda
- 2 tsp mixed spice
- 1 orange, zested
- 2 eggs
- 150ml cold pressed sunflower oil
- 200g carrots, grated

For the icing
- 100g butter, softened
- 300g soft cheese
- 100g icing sugar, sifted
- 1 tsp vanilla extract

1 Heat the oven to 180C/160C fan/gas 4 and line a 12-hole muffin tin with cases. In a large mixing bowl, mix the sugar, flours, bicarbonate of soda, mixed spice and orange zest, reserving a little zest to garnish. Whisk together the eggs and oil, then stir into the dry ingredients with the grated carrot. Divide the mixture into the cases and bake for 20–22 mins until a skewer poked in comes out clean. Cool on a wire rack before icing.

2 For the icing, beat the butter until really soft, then beat in the soft cheese, icing sugar and vanilla. Use a palette or cutlery knife to swirl the icing on top of the cakes, then decorate with some orange zest, if you like.

Nutrition per cupcake:
Kcals 442, fat 32g, saturates 14g, carbs 38g, sugars 26g, fibre 2g, protein 4g, salt 0.7g

Sticky ginger skillet parkin

Try this one-pan pud/cake hybrid for Bonfire Night, Halloween or cooler nights. Serve straight from the oven with cold cream. Don't use blackstrap molasses as that is too bitter.

PREP 10 mins plus cooling   COOK 50 mins   10-12

- 200g salted butter, chopped
- 85g light brown soft sugar
- 85g molasses
- 185g honey
- 250g self-raising flour
- 2 tsp ground ginger
- 1 tsp mixed spice
- 100g porridge oats
- 2 large eggs
- 2 tbsp milk
- 2 balls stem ginger from a jar, chopped, plus 2 tbsp syrup from the jar, and extra to serve
- cream, to serve (optional)

1 Heat the oven to 150C/130C fan/gas 2. Put a heavy-bottomed 25cm ovenproof frying pan or skillet over a low heat and gently melt the butter, sugar, molasses and honey together, stirring with a wooden spoon, until the butter is just melted and everything is combined. Remove from the heat and leave to cool slightly for 5–10 mins.

2 Sieve the flour and spices together, then mix in the oats. Whisk the eggs, milk, stem ginger and ginger syrup together in a bowl or jug. Stir the dry ingredients into the cooled butter mixture until well combined. Stir in the ginger, milk and egg mixture until you have a thick cake batter. Transfer to the oven and bake for 45–50 mins until firm and risen. Serve scooped from the pan with extra ginger syrup and cream, if you like, or leave to cool and eat cold. Will keep, wrapped in baking parchment, for up to 7 days.

Nutrition per serving (12):
Kcals 357, fat 16g, saturates 9g, carbs 48g, sugars 26g, fibre 2g, protein 5g, salt 0.55g

Fudgy coconut brownies

Dense and gooey, these store cupboard treats are made with cocoa rather than chocolate. Using cocoa powder makes them UPF-free and a great alternative to anything shop-bought.

PREP 10 mins   COOK 50 mins   Makes 16 brownies

- 100g cocoa powder
- 250g butter
- 500g golden caster sugar
- 4 eggs, beaten
- 100g self-raising flour
- 100g desiccated coconut
- icing sugar, to dust
  (optional)

1 Heat the oven to 180C/160C fan/gas 4. Line the base of a 21cm square tin with baking parchment. Put the cocoa, butter and sugar in your largest saucepan and gently melt, stirring so the mixture doesn't catch. When the cocoa mixture is melted and combined, cool slightly, then stir in the eggs, little by little, followed by the flour and coconut.

2 Tip into the tin and bake for 45 mins on a middle shelf – check after 30 mins and cover with another piece of baking parchment if the crust is browning too much. Cool in the tin, then carefully lift out and cut into squares.

Nutrition per brownie:
Kcals 358, fat 21g, saturates 13g, carbs 43g, sugars 35g, fibre 2g, protein 3g, salt 0.39g

Ultimate plum & apple cobbler

Slide this pudding into the oven after the Sunday roast has come out. It's classic comfort food and the cobbler topping can be used on any stewed fruit.

PREP 45 mins   COOK 40 mins   8–10

For the fruit
- 100g butter, cubed
- 100g golden caster sugar
- 2 vanilla pods, seeds scraped out
- 700g firm plums, stoned and roughly chopped
- 300g Braeburn apples, peeled, cored and chopped
- 1 tsp ground cinnamon

For the cobbler dough
- 1 egg
- 100ml milk
- 140g cold butter, cut into cubes
- 280g plain flour
- 140g golden caster sugar
- ½ tsp ground cinnamon
- 1 tbsp baking powder
- 2 tbsp demerara sugar
- cream, to serve

1 For the fruit, put all the ingredients in a saucepan. Cook over a low heat, stirring until the butter has melted and the sugar has dissolved, then leave to simmer until you have a chunky fruit compote, then set aside.

2 Heat the oven to 190C/170C fan/gas 6. Whisk the egg into the milk and set aside. Rub the butter and the flour together until it has the texture of chunky breadcrumbs, then stir in the caster sugar, cinnamon, baking powder and a large pinch of salt. Pour in the milk mixture and bring together to form a thick, batter-like texture.

3 Tip the compote into a baking dish and top with large spoonfuls of the cobbler mix, making sure there are a few gaps for the fruit to bubble through, then sprinkle everything with the demerara sugar. Bake for 35–40 mins or until the topping is golden and just cooked through. Remove from the oven and leave to rest for 5 mins before serving straight from the dish with a generous pour of cream.

Nutrition per serving (10):
Kcals 454, fat 21g, saturates 13g, carbs 60g, sugars 38g, fibre 3g, protein 5g, salt 0.8g

Blackberry & lemon fool

Create this delicious pudding in just 10 minutes, then pop it in the fridge. Serve in glasses and garnish with fresh blackberries for an elegant summer dessert.

 PREP 5 mins plus chilling   COOK 5 mins   2

- 200g blackberries, plus extra for the topping
- 3 tbsp icing sugar
- ½ lemon, zested and juiced
- 250ml double cream

1 Tip the blackberries into a pan with 2 tbsp icing sugar, plus the lemon zest and juice. Simmer until syrupy, then leave to cool. Chill for a few hours.

2 Whip the double cream with 1 tbsp icing sugar, then swirl through most of the blackberry sauce. Serve in glasses with extra sauce and fresh blackberries on top.

Nutrition per serving:
Kcals 744, fat 67g, saturates 42g, carbs 29g, sugars 29g, fibre 4g, protein 3g, salt 0.1g

Oaty apple crumble

This comforting pud combines juicy apples and sultanas with a crisp oat crumble topping.
Our recipe makes enough for 2 dishes, so you can freeze one ahead.

PREP 25 mins   COOK 1 hr 10 mins–1 hr 20 mins   10

- 6 Bramley apples, peeled, cored and cut into chunks
- 6 eating apples, peeled, cored and cut into chunks
- 85g caster sugar
- 100g sultanas or raisins
- 100g light brown soft sugar
- 50g honey
- 250g butter
- 300g porridge oats
- 300g plain flour
- 100g flaked almonds
- 1 tsp ground cinnamon

1 Cook the apples with the caster sugar in a large pan, stirring occasionally – add a splash of water if they start to stick on the bottom. When just about tender and a bit saucy, stir in the sultanas or raisins and tip into 2 large ovenproof dishes.

2 Melt the brown sugar, honey and butter together in a large pan. Off the heat, stir in the oats, flour, almonds and cinnamon until sticky and crumbly. Divide over the apples. To bake straight away, heat the oven to 180C/160C fan/gas 4, then bake for 40–50 mins until the topping is golden and crisp. To freeze, wrap the dishes well or freeze the fruit and crumble mixture in separate freezer bags if you don't have spare baking dishes. To cook from frozen, cover with foil and bake at 180C/160C fan/gas 4 for 1½ hrs, then turn the oven up to 220C/200C fan/gas 8 and bake for a further 45 mins, removing the foil for the last 15 mins.

Nutrition per serving:
Kcals 646, fat 29g, saturates 14g, carbs 91g, sugars 48g, fibre 8g, protein 11g, salt 0.48g

Pumpkin muffins

Try these easy-to-bake cinnamon-spiced pumpkin muffins as a mid-morning snack. Use any leftover pumpkin purée in a soup or store in the freezer for more muffins.

PREP 15 mins plus cooling   COOK 35 mins   Makes 12 muffins

- 750g pumpkin or butternut squash
- 225g plain flour
- 2 tsp baking powder
- 1 tbsp ground cinnamon (or 2 tsp pumpkin spice)
- 100g caster sugar
- 50g light brown soft sugar
- 2 large eggs
- 125g salted butter, melted

1 To steam the pumpkin, peel and seed it, then cut into evenly sized cubes. Put the cubes in a steamer or colander set over a pan of simmering water and cook for 10 mins. Test with the point of a knife and cook for a further 5 mins if not cooked through. Mash and leave to cool. Alternatively, to microwave the pumpkin, cut it in half (no need to peel it or cut out the seeds) and sit cut-side up in the microwave. Cook for 20 mins, then check the flesh is soft by poking it with a fork. Keep cooking if you'd like it softer. Scoop the flesh into a bowl, then mash and leave to cool completely.

2 Heat the oven to 200C/180C fan/gas 6. Line a 12-hole muffin tin with muffin cases. Mix the flour, baking powder, cinnamon and both sugars together in a large bowl. Break up any lumps of brown sugar by rubbing them between your fingers.

3 Whisk 200g of the pumpkin purée and eggs together in a jug, then add to the dry ingredients with the melted butter. Whisk for 1–2 mins with an electric hand whisk until just combined.

4 Bake for 15 mins until golden and risen and a skewer inserted comes out clean. Lift onto a wire rack to cool completely. Will keep for 3 days in an airtight container.

Nutrition per muffin:
Kcals 219, fat 10g, saturates 6g, carbs 28g, sugars 13g, fibre 2g, protein 4g, salt 0g

Banana peel loaf cake

Use every part of the banana in this clever breakfast loaf. Check the peanut butter only has peanuts and salt and make sure you buy vanilla extract and not essence to avoid any UPFs.

PREP 25 mins plus cooling   COOK 1 hr   10–12

- 125g salted butter, softened, plus extra for the tin
- 4 very ripe bananas
- 200g golden caster sugar
- 2 eggs, beaten
- 2 tsp vanilla extract
- 100ml Greek-style yogurt
- 300g white spelt flour or plain flour
- ½ tsp baking powder
- ½ tsp bicarbonate of soda
- 75g walnuts, roughly chopped

For the honey peanut butter
- 100g salted butter, softened
- 3 tbsp runny honey
- 3 tbsp smooth peanut butter

1 Heat the oven to 180C/160C fan/gas 4. Butter and line a 900g loaf tin. Trim the ends of the bananas and discard. Roughly chop the bananas, peel and all. Place in a food processor or blender and blitz until smooth. Tip into a bowl and set aside.

2 Using an electric hand whisk or stand mixer, beat together the butter and sugar with a pinch of salt until light and creamy, around 4–5 mins. Beat in the eggs, one at a time, then add the vanilla, yogurt and banana. Mix in the flour, baking powder and bicarb until combined. Fold through the walnuts and gently spoon the batter into the prepared tin. Bake for 50–60 mins until a skewer inserted into the middle comes out clean. Transfer to a wire rack and leave to cool in the tin for 15 mins before removing from the tin and leaving to cool completely.

3 For the honey peanut butter, beat all the ingredients together using an electric hand whisk or stand mixer until creamy. Cut the cake into slices and spread over the butter. The butter and cake will keep in airtight containers for 5 days.

Nutrition per serving (12):
Kcals 430, fat 24g, saturates 12g, carbs 45g, sugars 27g, fibre 2g, protein 8g, salt 0.6g

Cinnamon rolls

Prepare these the day before for warm, sticky buns for breakfast. Make sure you're buying vanilla extract not essence and check the soft cheese ingredients to avoid UPFs.

PREP 40 mins plus at least 2 hrs 30 mins resting and proving   COOK 40 mins   Makes 12 rolls

For the dough
- 500g strong white bread flour, plus extra for dusting
- 7g sachet fast-action dried yeast
- 1 tsp ground cinnamon
- 50g golden caster sugar
- 200ml warm milk
- 2 eggs
- 100g butter, softened, plus extra for the tin
- 2 tbsp honey

For the filling
- 150g light brown soft sugar
- 2 tbsp ground cinnamon
- 125g butter, at room temperature

For the icing
- 50g soft cheese
- 50g icing sugar
- ¼ tsp vanilla extract

1 Tip all the ingredients for the dough, except the butter and honey, into the bowl of a stand mixer with 1 tsp salt. Use the paddle attachment to combine into a dough, then tip out onto a floured surface and knead for 2 mins until smooth. Put back in the bowl and gradually add the butter, 1–2 tsp at a time, while mixing on a medium setting. Flatten to a 20 x 20cm square, then cover and freeze for 30 mins.

2 Meanwhile, butter and line the base and sides of a deep 20 x 30cm baking tray. To make the filling, mix the sugar with the cinnamon and a large pinch of sea salt, then set aside 2 tbsp. Beat in the butter to form a paste.

3 Lay the dough on a floured surface and roll to a neat 35 x 25cm rectangle. Spread over the filling so it's completely covered. Fold the bottom third of the dough into the middle, then fold over again to cover the top third. For the best results, chill the dough again for another 30 mins.

4 Re-roll the dough to another rectangle about 40 x 30cm, then roll it up along the long edge into a tight log. To get the neatest spirals, cut in half, lift onto a tray and freeze for 15 mins to firm up, then cut into 12 equal-sized slices. Arrange the slices, spiral-side up, in the tin. Leave to prove in the fridge for at least 1 hr, or up to 24 hrs.

5 Heat the oven to 200C/180C fan/gas 6. Bake the buns for 20 mins, then scatter over the reserved cinnamon sugar and bake for 10–15 mins until deep brown.

6 Meanwhile, mix the honey with 2 tsp boiling water. As soon as the buns come out of the oven, brush them with the syrup glaze, then leave to cool a little. To make the icing, beat the soft cheese, icing sugar and vanilla together, then gradually add 1–2 tbsp boiling water to create a thick but pourable consistency. Drizzle the icing over the buns.

Nutrition per roll:
Kcals 421, fat 18g, saturates 11g, carbs 55g, sugars 24g, fibre 2g, protein 8g, salt 0.9g

Lemon drizzle sponge pudding

Transform a classic lemon drizzle cake into a self-saucing pud for a cheap, comforting dessert. Serve with cream or custard.

PREP 15 mins   COOK 50 mins   10

- 250g butter, softened, plus extra for the dish
- 380g caster sugar
- 4 eggs
- 250g self-raising flour
- 1 tsp baking powder
- 3 lemons, zested and juiced
- 2½ tbsp cornflour
- double cream, to serve

For the drizzle
- 50g icing sugar
- 1 lemon, zested and juiced

1 Heat the oven to 180C/160C fan/gas 4. Butter a 30 x 20cm deep baking dish.

2 Put the butter and 250g caster sugar in a bowl and beat for 5 mins until pale and fluffy. Whisk in the eggs, then sieve over the flour and baking powder and fold in until you have a batter. Stir in the lemon zest, reserving a little for decoration.

3 Spoon the sponge batter into the dish and smooth over the top.

4 Mix the lemon juice with the cornflour in a heatproof bowl to make a smooth paste. Mix the remaining 130g caster sugar with 300ml boiling water in a jug, pour over the cornflour mix and whisk until smooth. Pour this over the sponge. Bake for 45–50 mins until golden and set, and the sponge springs back when touched.

5 While the pudding is baking, make the lemon drizzle. Mix the icing sugar with enough lemon juice (about half of it) to create a loose consistency. Drizzle over the sponge while it's still warm and decorate with the reserved lemon zest. Serve straightaway with cream.

Nutrition per serving:
Kcals 492, fat 23g, saturates 14g, carbs 66g, sugars 43g, fibre 1g, protein 5g, salt 0.9g

Dorset apple traybake

Simple-to-make apple cake that can be cut into bars or squares for a teatime treat. Make sure you check that you're buying vanilla extract and not essence to avoid any UPFs.

PREP 20 mins COOK 50 mins Makes 16 bars

- 225g butter, softened, plus extra for the tin
- 450g cooking apples (such as Bramley)
- ½ lemon, juiced
- 280g golden caster sugar
- 4 eggs
- 2 tsp vanilla extract
- 350g self-raising flour
- 2 tsp baking powder
- demerara sugar, to sprinkle

1 Heat the oven to 180C/160C fan/gas 4. Butter and line a rectangular baking tin (approx 27 x 20cm) with baking parchment. Peel, core and thinly slice the apples, then squeeze over the lemon juice. Set aside.

2 Put the butter, caster sugar, eggs, vanilla, flour and baking powder into a large bowl and mix well until smooth. Spread half the mixture into the prepared tin. Arrange half the apples over the top of the mixture, then repeat the layers. Sprinkle over the demerara sugar.

3 Bake for 45–50 mins until golden and springy to the touch. Leave to cool for 10 mins, then turn out of the tin and remove the paper. Cut into bars or squares.

Nutrition per bar:
Kcals 285, fat 13g, saturates 8g, carbs 39g, sugars 23g, fibre 1g, protein 4g, salt 0.7g

Bramley & blackberry pie

Make the most of seasonal fruit in this pie. Using a metal or enamel pie dish will ensure your base is crispy. If you're feeling fancy, stamp out and layer small circles for the topping.

PREP 50 mins plus macerating and chilling   COOK 45 mins   6–8

For the pastry
- 225g cold unsalted butter, chopped into small pieces
- 350g plain flour
- 50g icing sugar
- 1 large egg yolk (save the white for brushing the pastry)

For the filling
- 900g Bramley apples (about 4), peeled, cored, quartered and thinly sliced
- 140g golden caster sugar, plus extra for sprinkling
- 1 tbsp fine polenta or ground almonds
- 1 tbsp cornflour or plain flour, plus extra for dusting
- 1½ tsp ground cinnamon
- 200g blackberries, halved if very large
- egg white, for brushing (reserved from making the pastry)
- cream, to serve

1 For the pastry, put the butter and flour in a food processor with ¼ tsp salt and blend until the mixture resembles damp breadcrumbs. Add the sugar and briefly whizz again. Whisk the egg yolk with 2 tbsp cold water and drizzle over the flour. Use the pulse button to blend the mixture until it starts to form larger clumps. If the mixture seems too dry, add a little more water a tsp at a time, but no more than 3 tsp. Tip out onto a work surface and briefly knead to bring it into a smooth ball. Flatten into a round and cover. Chill for at least 30 mins or up to 2 days.

2 Next, make the filling. Put the apples and half the sugar in a large bowl, then stir together until the apples are well coated. Set aside for 30 mins to macerate.

3 Remove the dough from the fridge and cut in 2 pieces, one slightly larger than the other. Cover the small piece and set aside. Divide the larger piece into the number of pies you'd like to make or leave whole for a large one. On a lightly floured surface, roll out to the thickness of a 50p piece or until large enough to line the base of your pie dish, with a little pastry overhang. Roll the dough over your rolling pin, lift onto your dish, then press it well into the corners. Scatter the polenta or almonds over the base.

4 Heat the oven to 190C/170C fan/gas 5 and put a baking sheet on the middle shelf. Drain any juice from the apples, then stir in the remaining sugar, cornflour and cinnamon. Layer the apples and blackberries in the lined dish, creating a dome effect. Roll out the remaining piece of dough, until just big enough to cover your dish with a little overhang. Trim the edges and crimp the sides together using your hands or a fork. Whisk the egg white and brush over the top. Scatter with the extra sugar, then put on the baking sheet. Bake for 35–45 mins, until the pastry is golden and crisp and juices bubbling. Cool for 10 mins before serving with cream.

Nutrition per serving (8):
Kcals 543, fat 25g, saturates 15g, carbs 70g, sugars 36g, fibre 5g, protein 6g, salt 0.2g

Index